INSPIRED TANGLES

A Book of Zentangles and Thoughtful Inspiration

Tiffany Taylor Wright

Balboa Press books may be ordered through booksellers or by contacting:

Balboa Press
A Division of Hay House
1663 Liberty Drive
Bloomington, IN 47403
www.balboapress.com
1 (877) 407-4847

Because of the dynamic nature of the Internet, any web addresses or links contained in this book may have changed since publication and may no longer be valid. The views expressed in this work are solely those of the author and do not necessarily reflect the views of the publisher, and the publisher hereby disclaims any responsibility for them.

Any people depicted in stock imagery provided by Thinkstock are models, and such images are being used for illustrative purposes only.
Certain stock imagery © Thinkstock.

ISBN: 978-1-5043-5034-1 (sc)
ISBN: 978-1-5043-5035-8 (e)

Library of Congress Control Number: 2016903056

Print information available on the last page.

Balboa Press rev. date: 06/25/2016

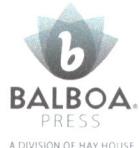

Introduction

I rarely share this part of my life with anyone as it is just so gut-wrenchingly painful and my heart breaks all over again, but through my pain, these drawings and this book evolved and took shape. I therefore felt that by sharing my story it would help you to better understand the healing and artistic journey I have been traveling while creating this book.

It was an incredibly hot Fresno afternoon on Tuesday, August 30, 2011. I was at the law firm where I worked when the phone rang at about 2:45 p.m. It was my daughter, Hayley, who was 14 years old at the time. She didn't quite sound like herself when she said "Mom, Hunter was supposed to pick me up after school today and he's not here yet." My kids both were attending Central High School, but as Hayley was a freshman, she attended the West campus which was in the country and my son, Hunter, was a junior attending the East Campus of Central High which was in town. Hayley said "Mom he's really late and I've been hearing a lot of sirens and have seen police cars and fire engines go by." She went on to say "Mom, I have a bad feeling that something has happened to Hunter, can you come get me right now?"

My co-worker, Pam was standing next me while I was on the phone. Her words were: "Just go now! Go!" God puts Angels in our paths at just the right times. I will be forever grateful to Pam for urging me to leave the office that day and go to the school to pick up Hayley and figure out what had happened.

I rushed to the school and once she was in the car, my cell phone rang. It was my ex-husband. He said that the school had called him and indicated that Hunter had been involved in a rollover accident, but they had no more information. I tried to remain calm and told myself that people walked away from rollovers all the time right? But I had an awful knot in my stomach and my heart was pounding hard.

The only other information the school was able to provide us was the name of the street where the accident had occurred, McKinley Avenue—no cross street. Hayley and I got on McKinley as fast as we could and started driving east. We were both steering as I got on the phone and called 911 and the highway patrol. We weren't seeing anything driving east, so I turned around and started west. I was still on the phone trying to get the location of the accident when we came to the road Rolinda and a huge roadblock. There must have been what seemed like 20 cars, police cars, firetrucks and emergency vehicles as well as a rescue helicopter hovering overhead. I drove through the cars blocking the road running over downed power lines, as Hunter's car had knocked the power pole completely over. A police officer made me turn around and go back. Once I turned around, we parked and got out of the car. Hunter's best friend's mom, Antonette came to me. Her son, Alfonso had also been in the car, as well as two other friends of Hunter's. Her son and the other boys had been taken to the hospital. Antonette had waited at the accident scene until I got there instead of going to the hospital with her son. Another one of God's Angels sent to me that day.

One of the principals of the school approached and stood before me. Everything was just a blur at this point, but I asked how the boys were. In the car had been Hunter and three of his friends on their way to pick up Hayley from school. The principle informed me that the three boys had been transported to the hospital with minor injuries, but my Hunter did not make it. I hugged Hayley tight and slid to the ground. This just could not be happening! Hayley and I were in shock.

There had been a bump in the road right at the intersection and Hunter was going too fast. After going over the bump he hit some gravel and couldn't regain control of the car. Hunter hit the power pole, rolled the car three times, went through a farmer's fence and into his yard landing upside down before coming to a stop under a tree.

Hunter was not wearing his seat belt. He had been killed instantly.

I remember standing there in the hot Fresno sun like it was yesterday, although the anniversary of Hunter's death is coming upon five years. I remember saying to Hayley and Antonette "God must have needed Hunter right this minute. He must have had a very important job for him to do." I just knew that deep in my heart.

A school official drove us back to the school and I called my fiancé, Scott who came to be with us. I had not called my ex-husband yet as I knew he was driving and didn't think it would be wise. I placed a phone call to my ex-mother-in-law and she and my ex-father-in-law came to the school as well. My ex-husband called and I could not put the inevitable off. I had the horrible task of telling him that Hunter had died in the crash. Devastation again.

I did not know how I was going to tell my parents. They were so close to Hunter, especially my dad. They were best friends. In the end, my ex-mother-in-law called them for me. I just could not do it. It was like living in a nighmare that I just couldn't wake up from.

The students put together a candlelight ceremony at the varsity baseball field. Hunter was on the varsity baseball team. He had absolutely loved and lived baseball from the age of five years old.

We planned the funeral, the notice came out in the paper, news articles were published and counselors were on both campuses for the students. Hunter was an extremely well-liked young man and touched the lives of most everyone he ever encountered. Hunter had many, many life experiences in his 17 years. I truly believe that Hunter accomplished everything that God had planned for him.

I saw Hunter the night before the accident. He lived with his father at the time and came over to see me. He came into my room, gave me one of his huge bear hugs and said "I love you mommy." I cling to that moment and think of it often. It gives me a certain amount of peace and comfort.

Hunter's funeral was one of the largest I've ever seen. There was standing room only and projected into two adjacent buildings of the church. Most of both high school campuses were there. Burying my child has been, and will always be, the most heart-wrenching thing I have ever done in my life. As I mentioned, it will be five years in August, that my son has been gone, but, my heart is still as broken as it was the day he died.

Thank you for allowing, me to share my story with you. This leads me to the present.

I needed an outlet for my grief, so when my mother brought home a zentangling book, a sketchbook and black ink pens for my daughter to work on over her summer break, I was very curious. After a time, I took over the book and supplies and never looked back. I practiced and drew every day for hours on end. I was hooked. I purchased every book on the subject I could get my hands on and my library and drawings grew and grew.

My zentangles started out using black ink only and were very free-form designs following the examples in the books I had purchased. I combined all sorts of different designs or "tangles" as they are referred to.

Creating these zentangle pieces has been, and continues to be, very cathartic for me in my grief and the continuing healing process of losing my son.

Eventually, I began using color to fill in the designs and loved the end result. I soon discovered watercolor pencils. Using the watercolor pencils and a handy water brush, I began using this technique and the results were very vibrant colors and a totally new look to my artwork. Many colored deigns later I became interested in hand lettering. I combined my new lettering with my watercolor pencils and all of a sudden, I had started a book.

I have created my watercolored, whimsical lettering in the form of the letters of the alphabet and my love of a great quotation to create this book.

I hope you will enjoy this book as much as I have enjoyed creating it.

- Tiffany Taylor Wright

Acknowledgement

This book would not have been possible had it not have been for the love and support of my mother and father, Bob and Jill Green and my daughter, Hayley. I would also like to acknowledge my son, Hunter, whose Spirit always surrounds me, giving me inspiration. Their love and constant encouragement has been, and continues to be, such a blessing to me.

Dedication

This book is dedicated to my loving son and Angel in Heaven, Hunter Scott Wright

(1994-2011)

and

To my beautiful and extraordinary daughter, Hayley Taylor Wright

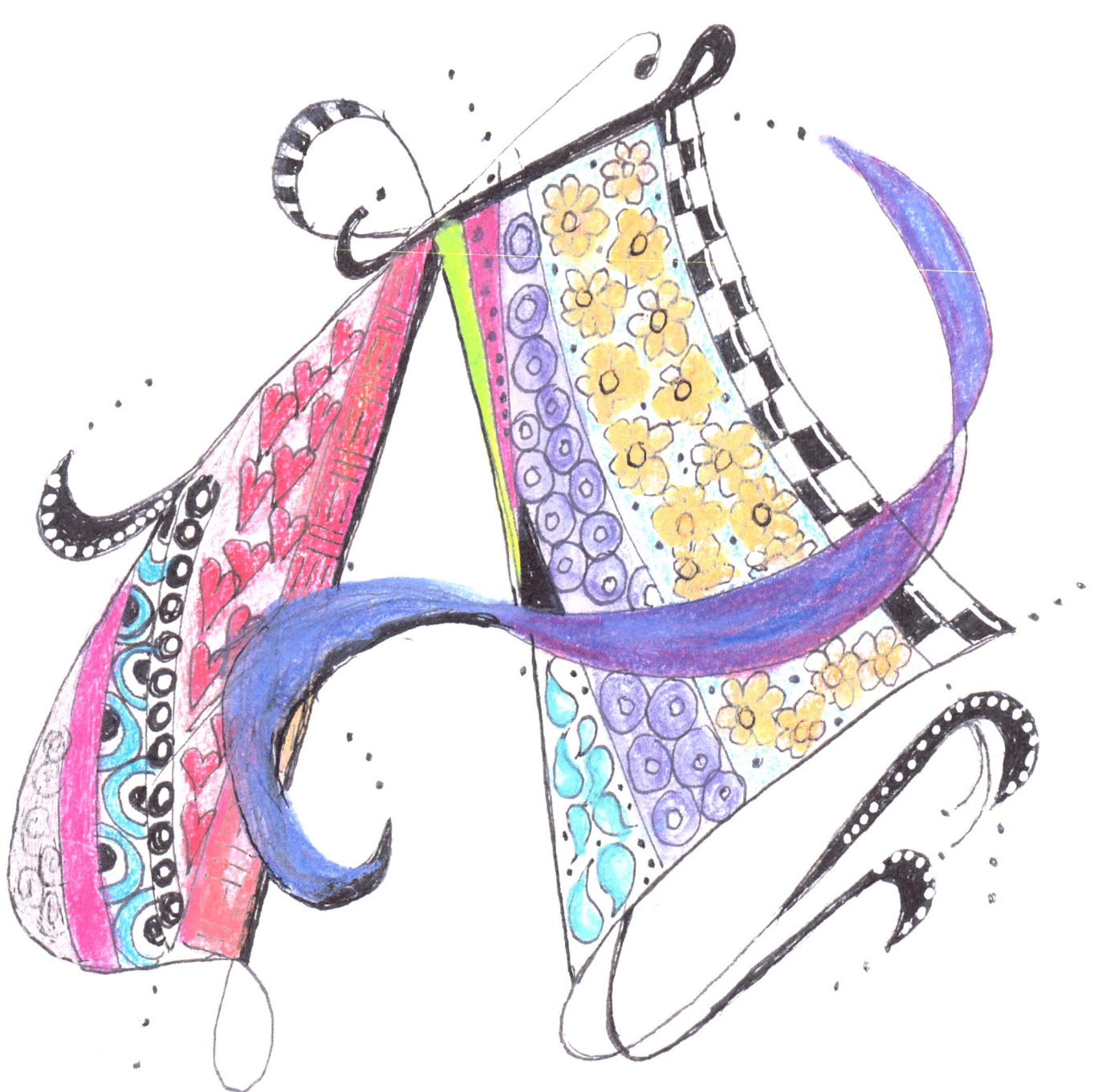

Do not carry the burden of the past, do not live in the future.

The only important thing is that one lives in the present AUTHENTICALLY and fully. Whatever your current life is, be the most you can be by living in the moment.

--Chan Chih

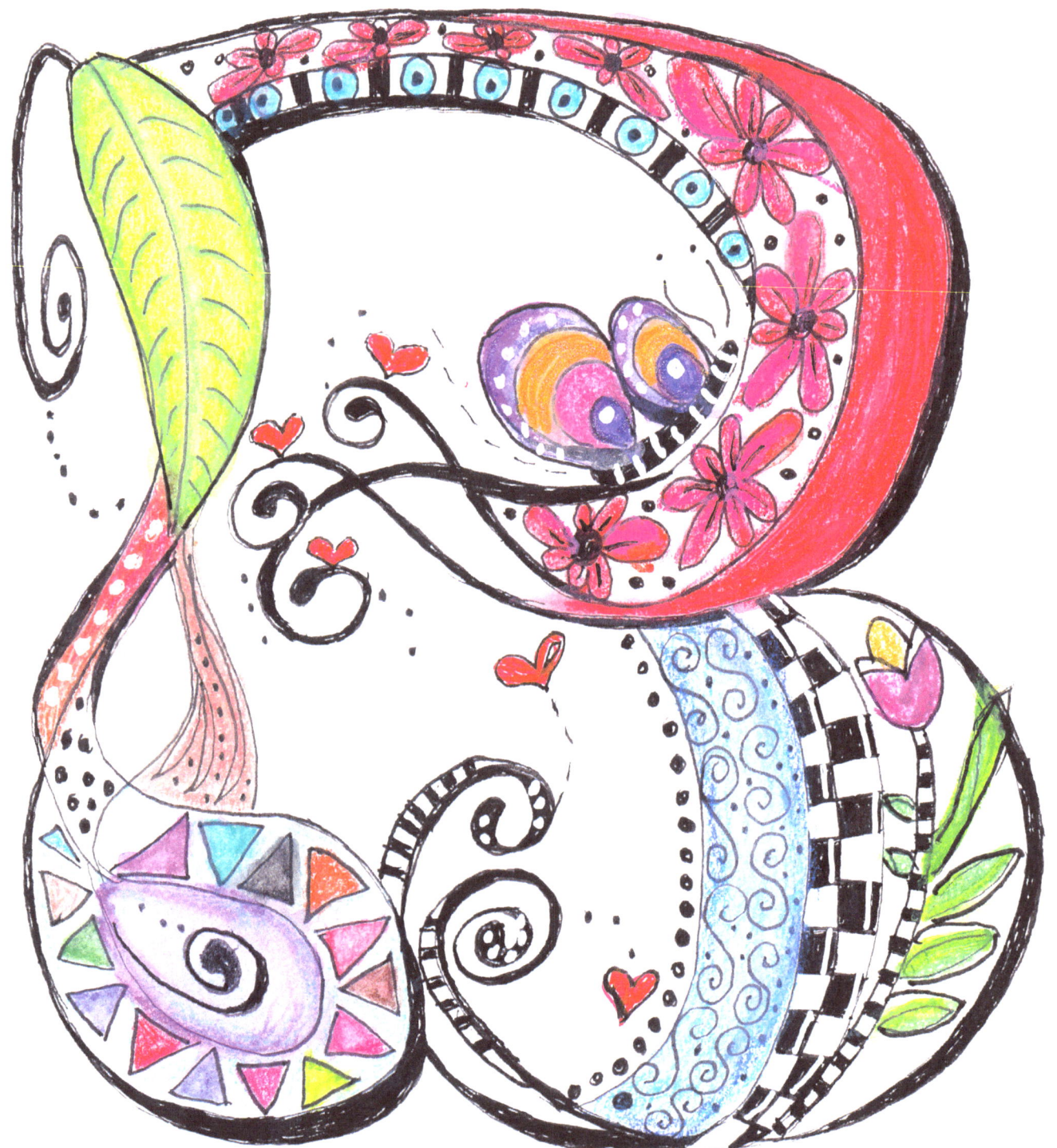

I BELIEVE in manicures.

I BELIEVE in overdressing.

I BELIEVE in primping at leisure and wearing lipstick.

I BELIEVE in pink.

I BELIEVE that laughing is the best calorie burner.

I BELIEVE in kissing a lot.

I BELIEVE in being strong when everything else seems to be going wrong.

I BELIEVE happy girls are the prettiest girls.

I BELIEVE tomorrow is another day.

I BELIEVE in miracles.

--Audrey Hepburn

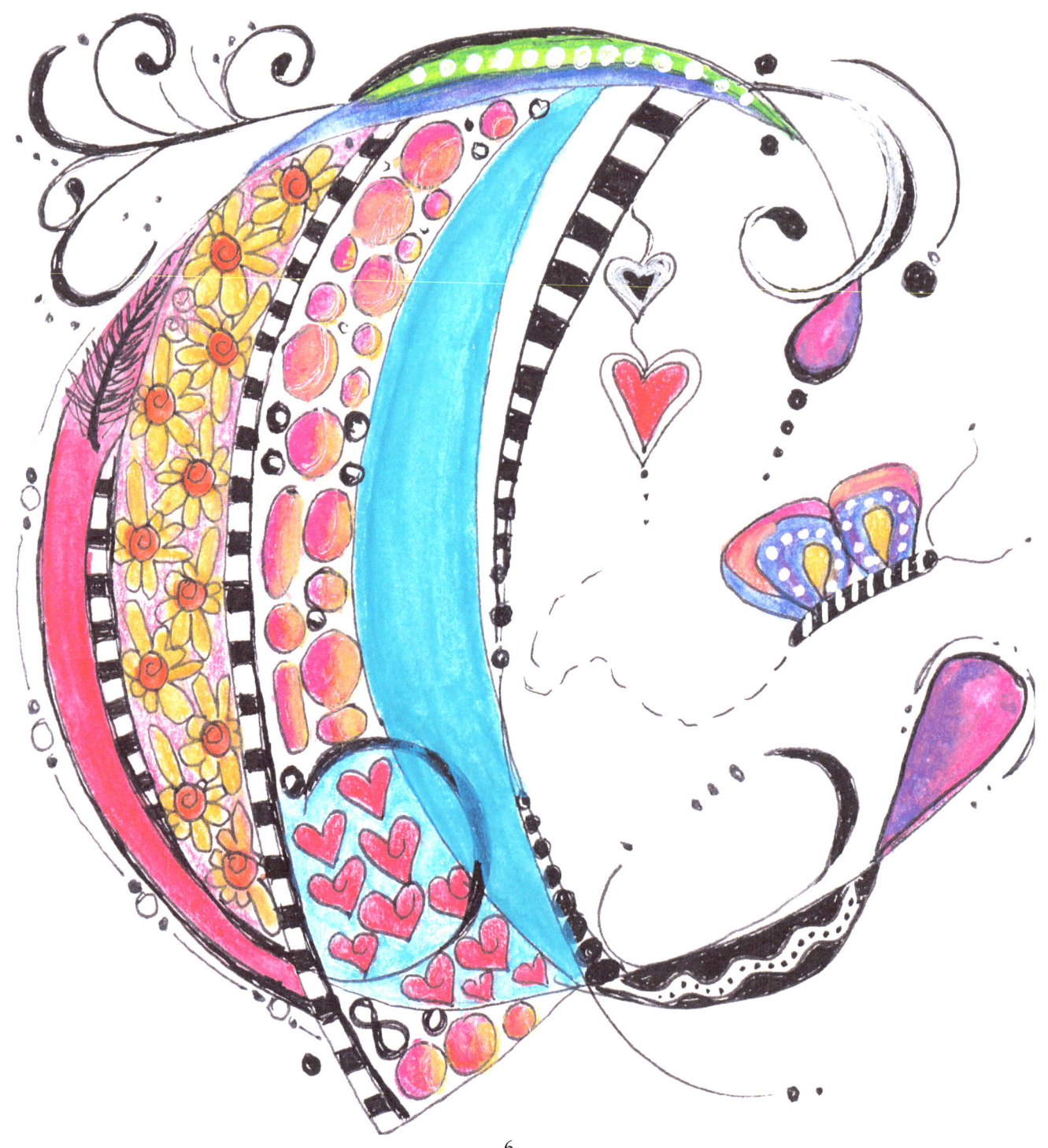

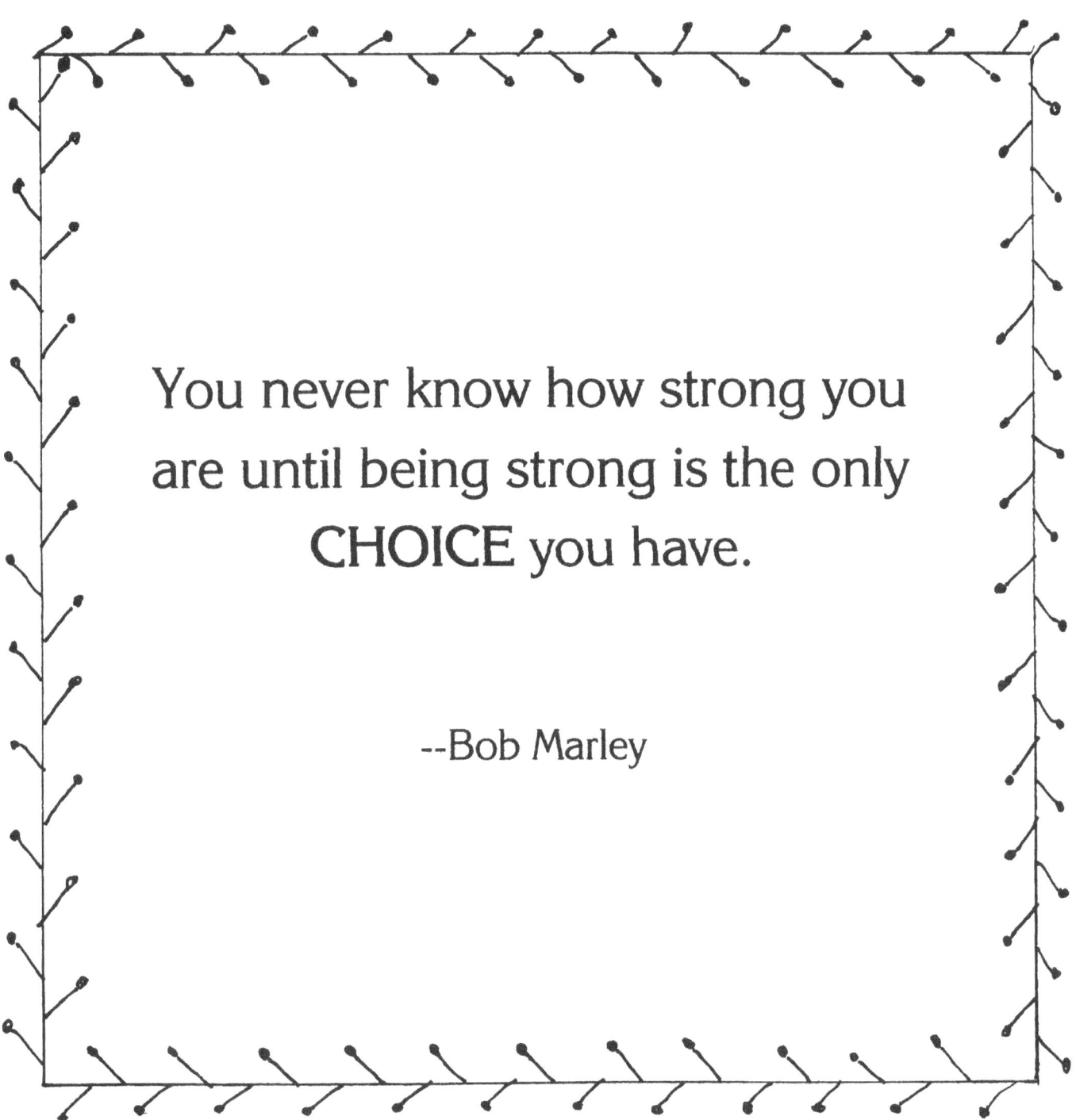

You never know how strong you are until being strong is the only **CHOICE** you have.

--Bob Marley

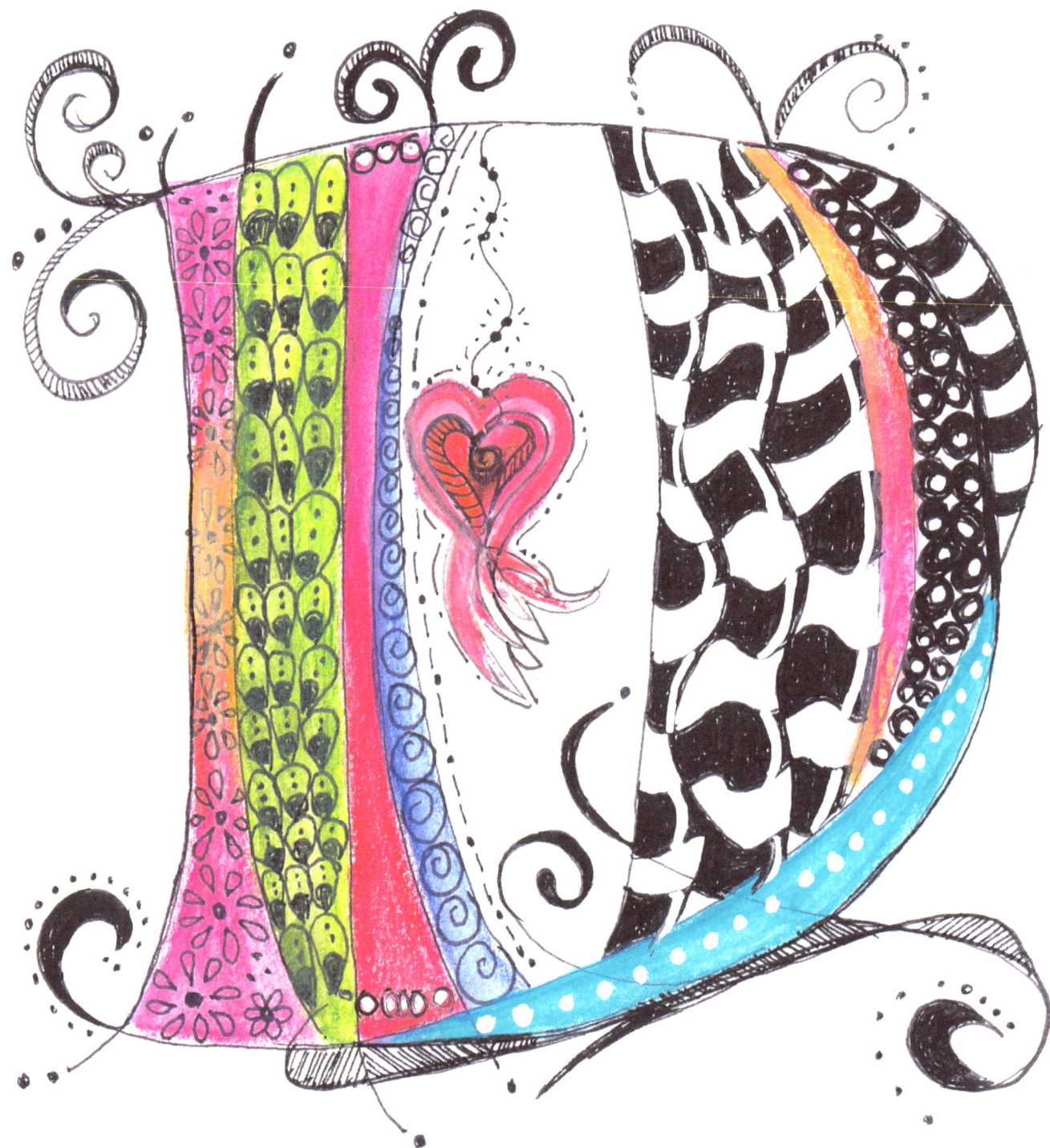

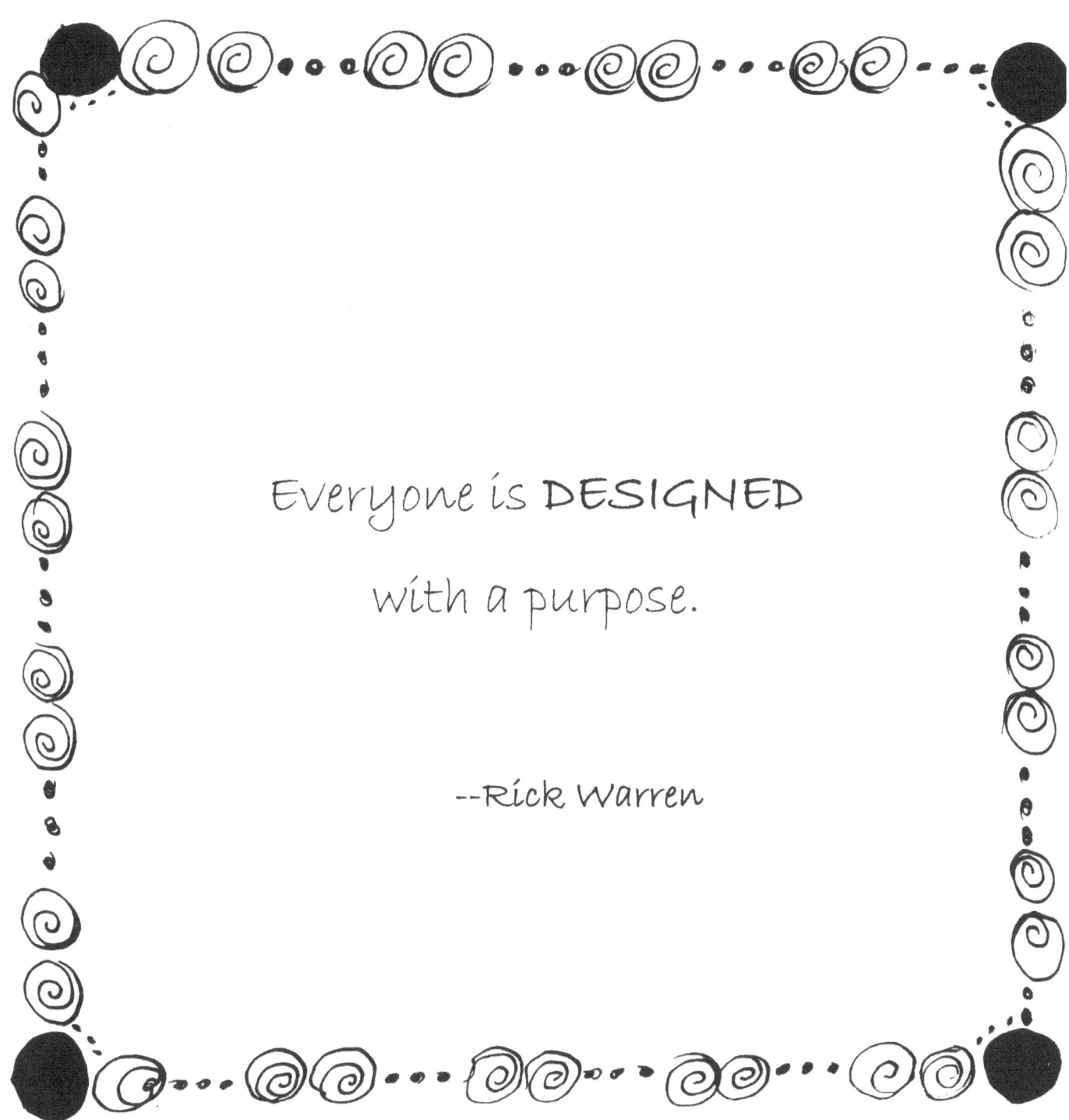

Everyone is **DESIGNED**

with a purpose.

--Rick Warren

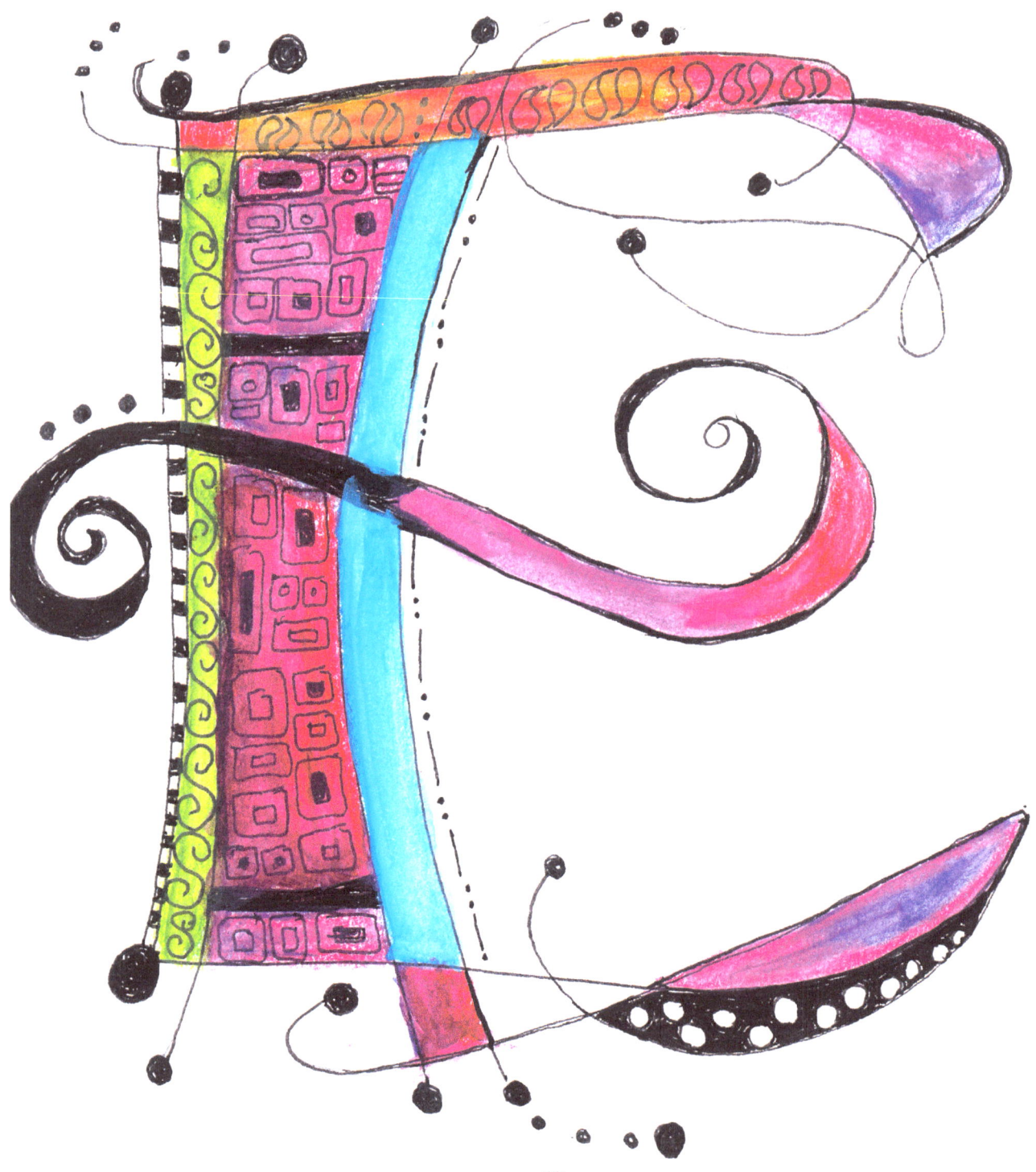

10

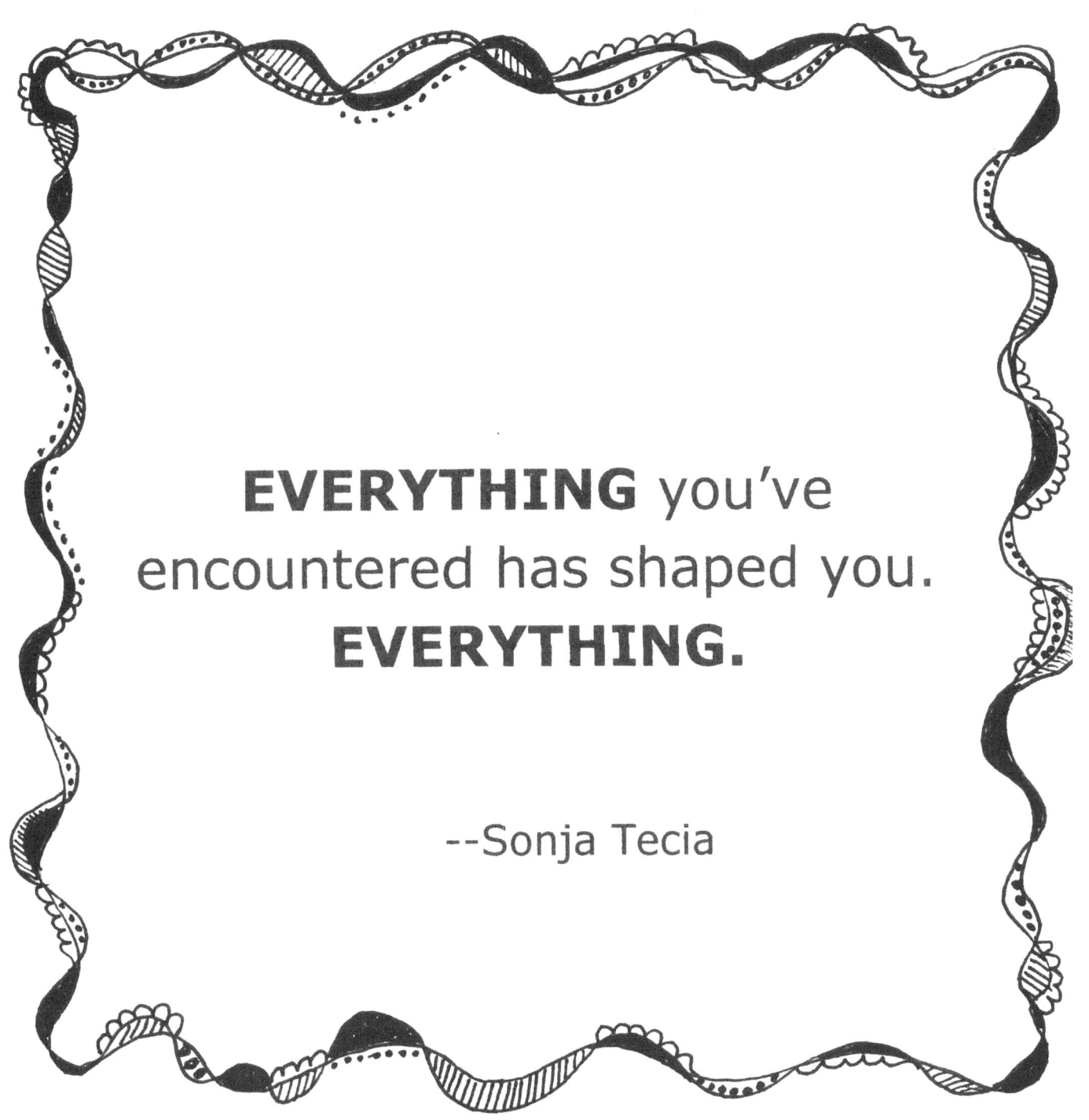

EVERYTHING you've encountered has shaped you. **EVERYTHING.**

--Sonja Tecia

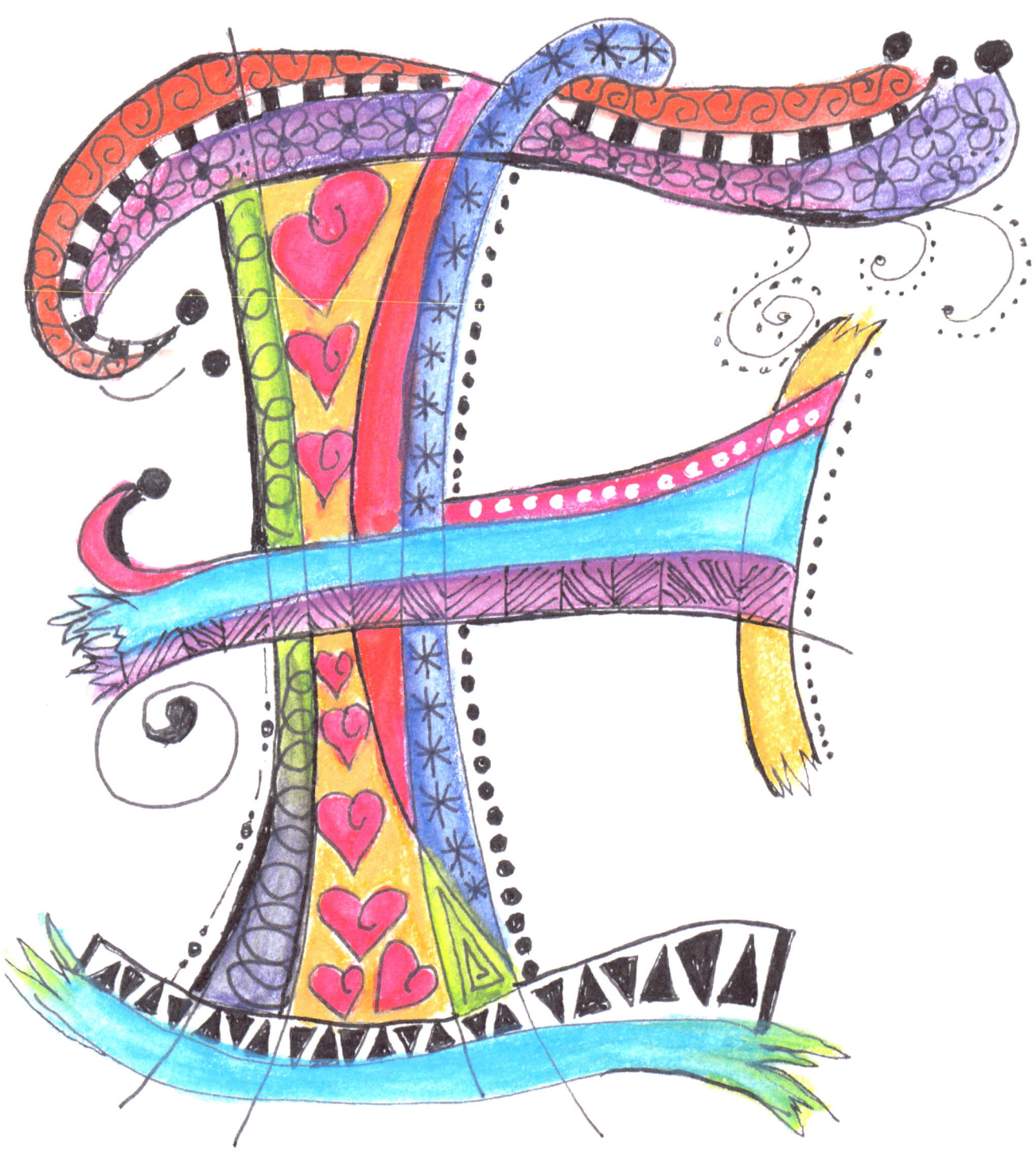

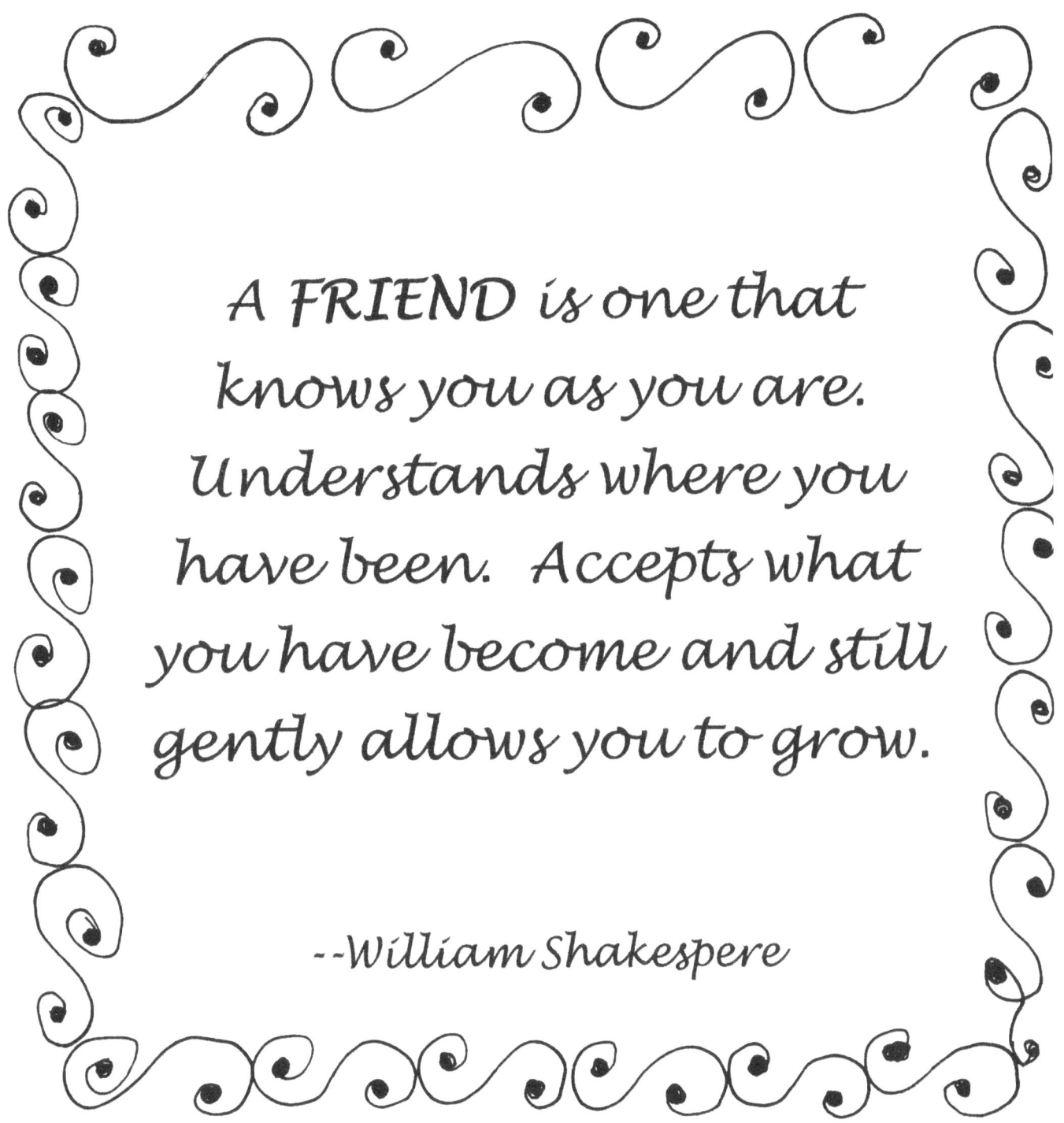

A *FRIEND* is one that knows you as you are. Understands where you have been. Accepts what you have become and still gently allows you to grow.

--William Shakespere

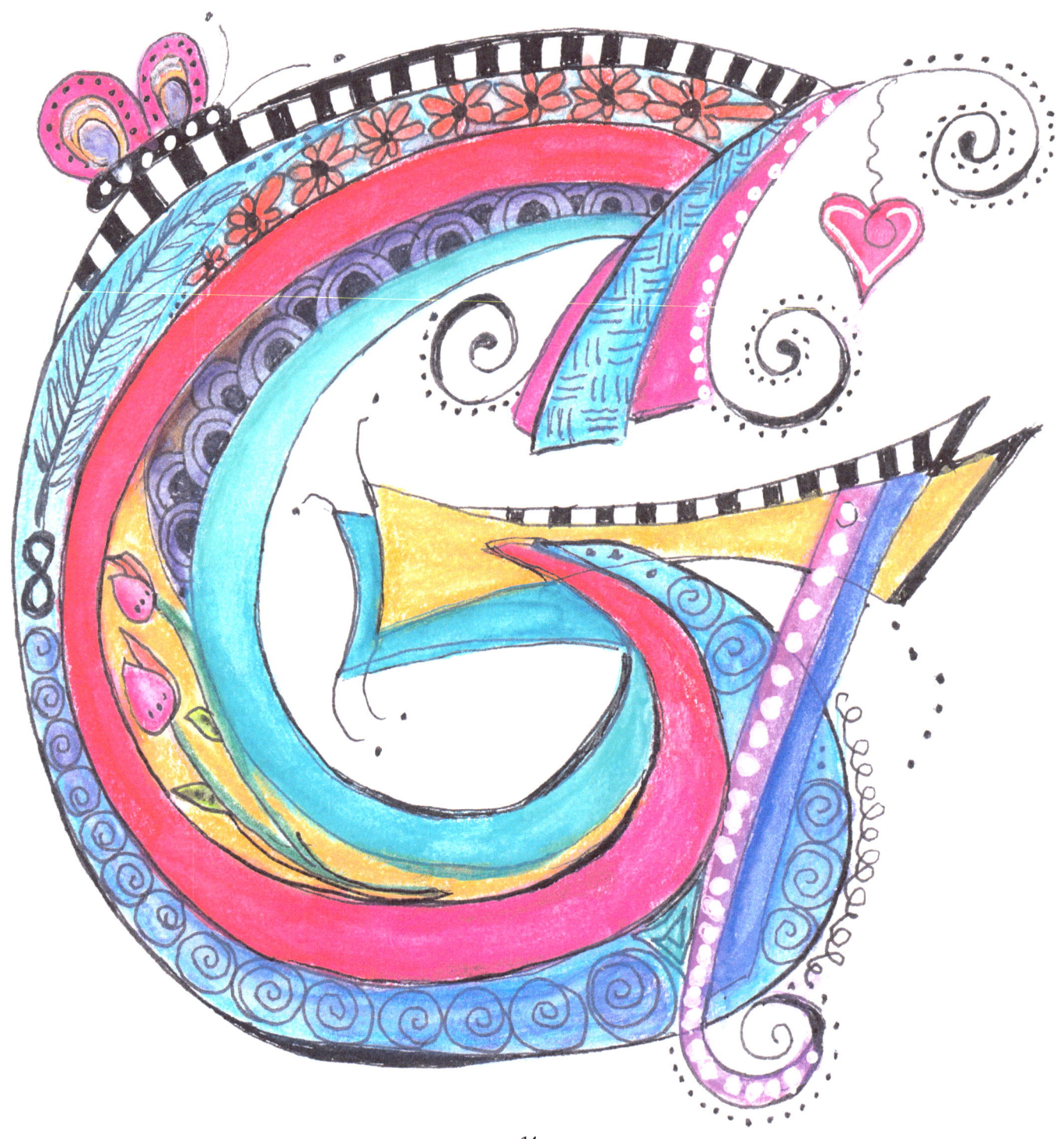

14

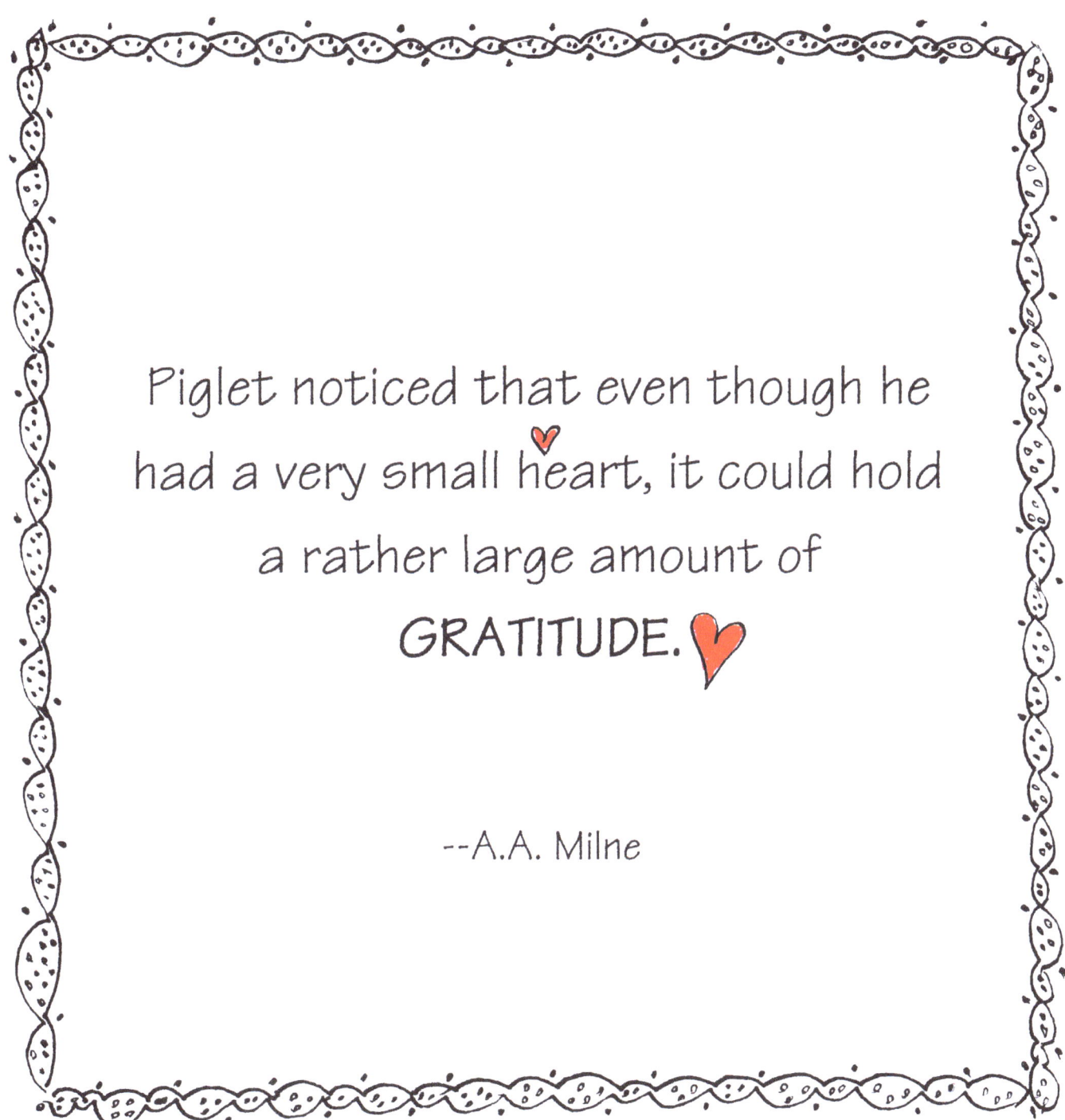

Piglet noticed that even though he
had a very small heart, it could hold
a rather large amount of
GRATITUDE.

--A.A. Milne

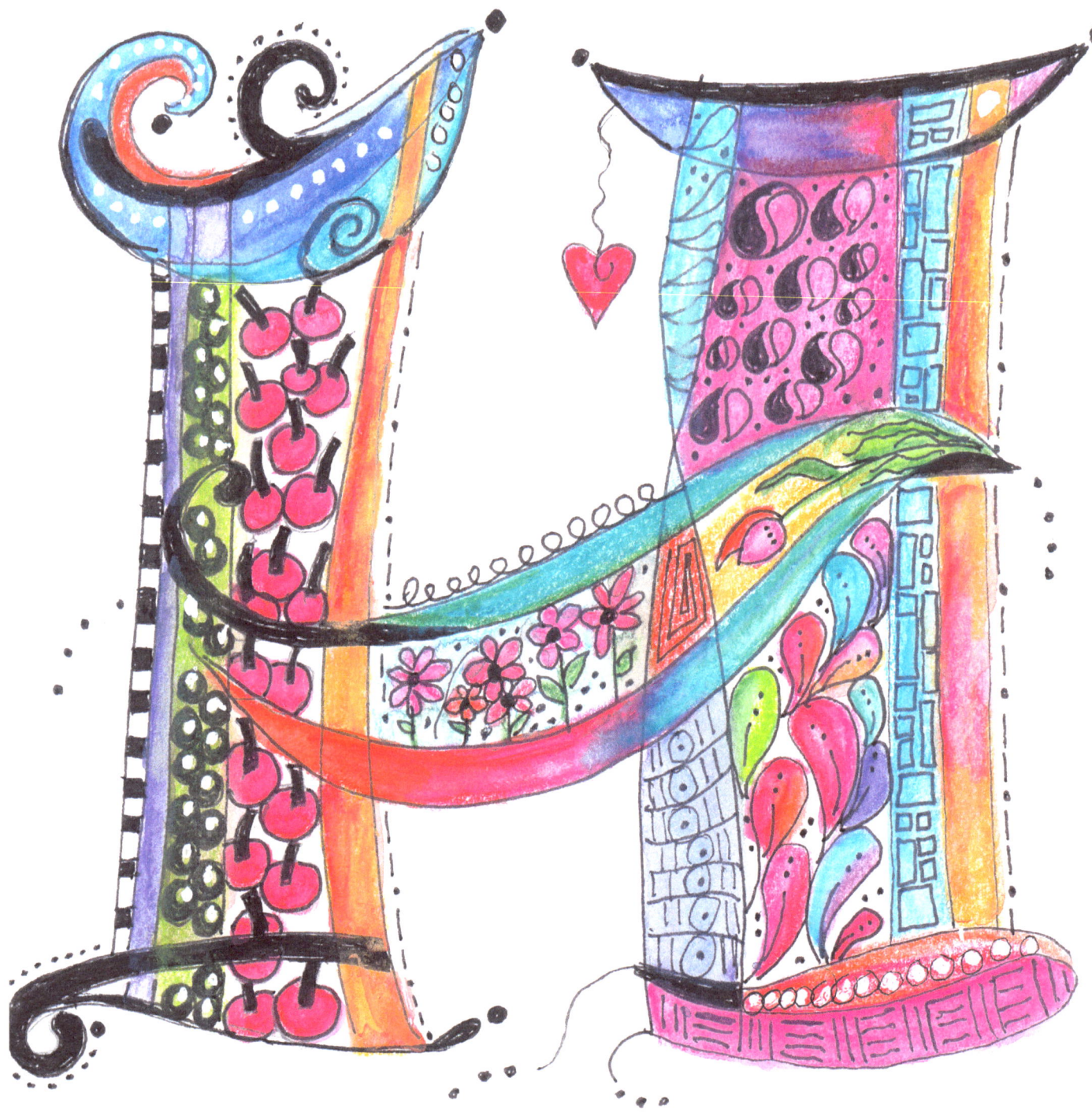

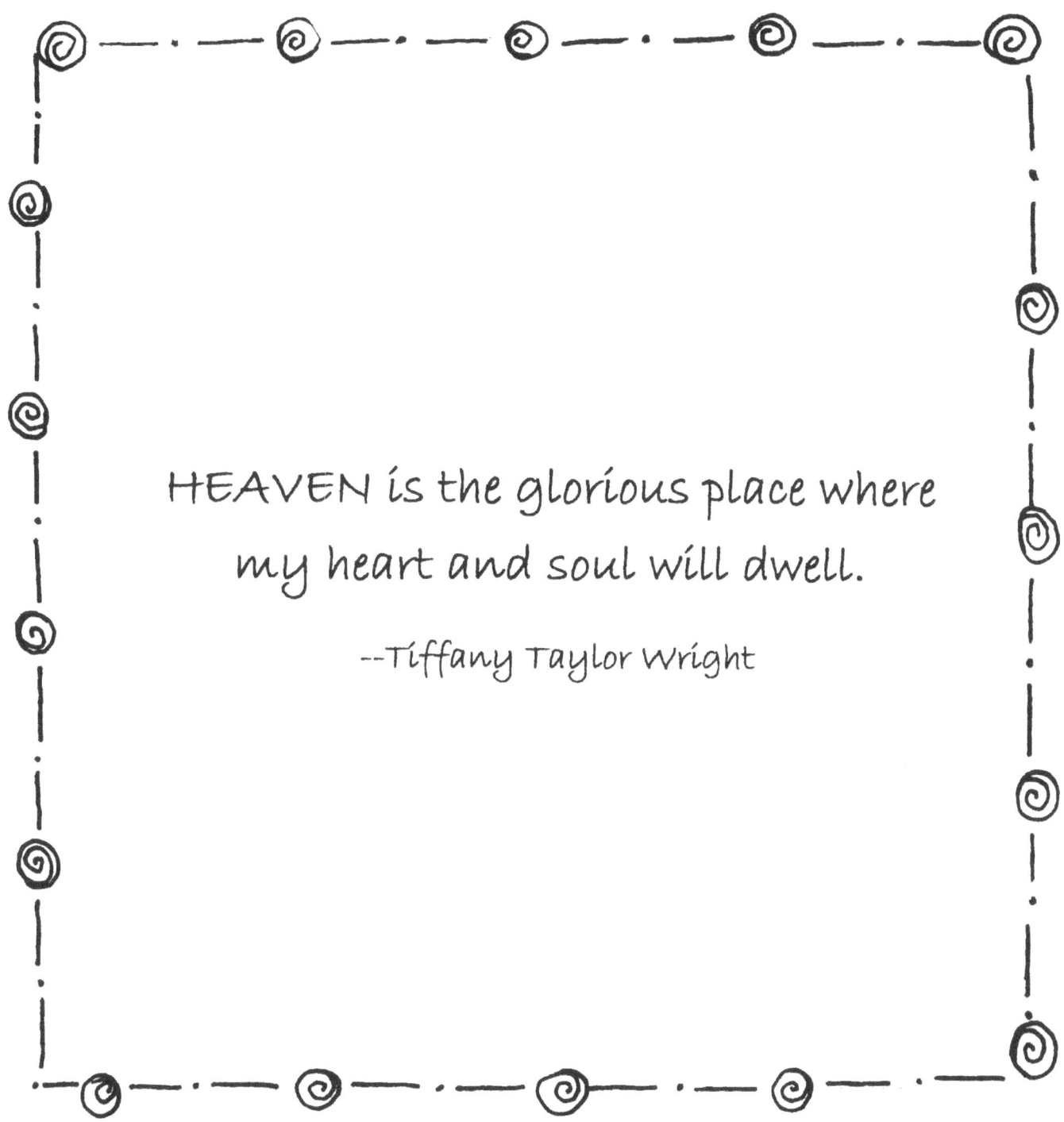

HEAVEN is the glorious place where
my heart and soul will dwell.

--Tiffany Taylor Wright

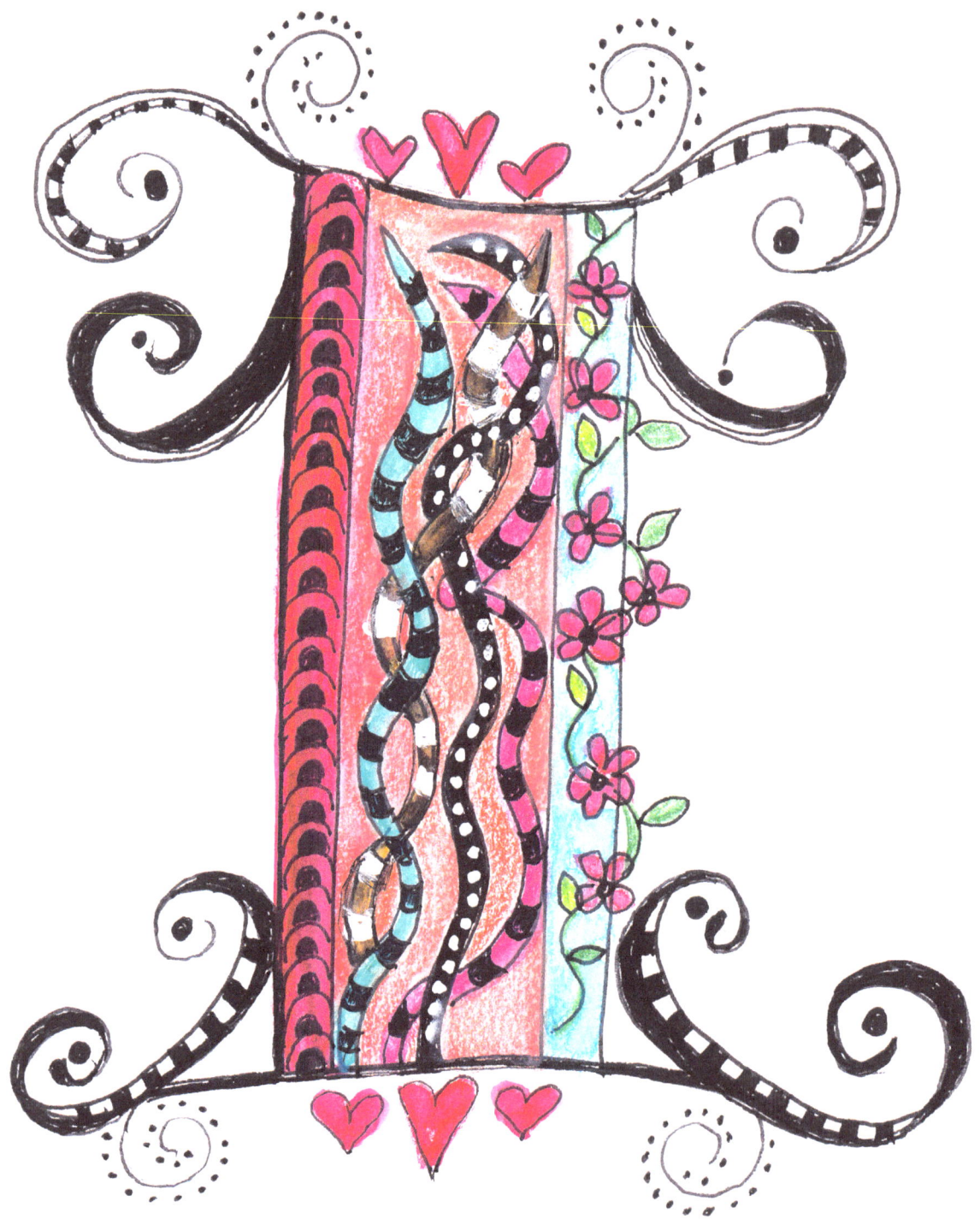

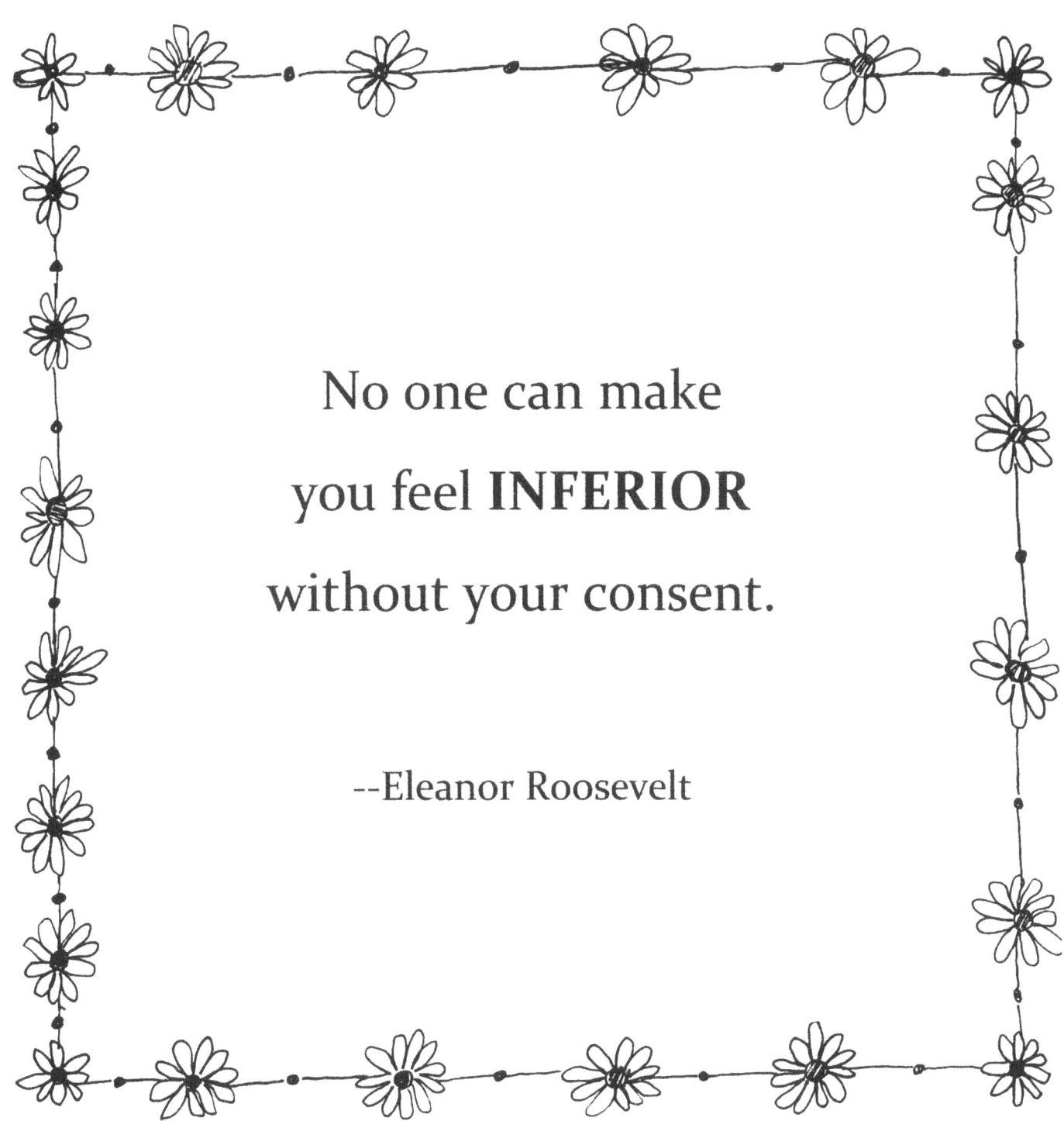

No one can make

you feel **INFERIOR**

without your consent.

--Eleanor Roosevelt

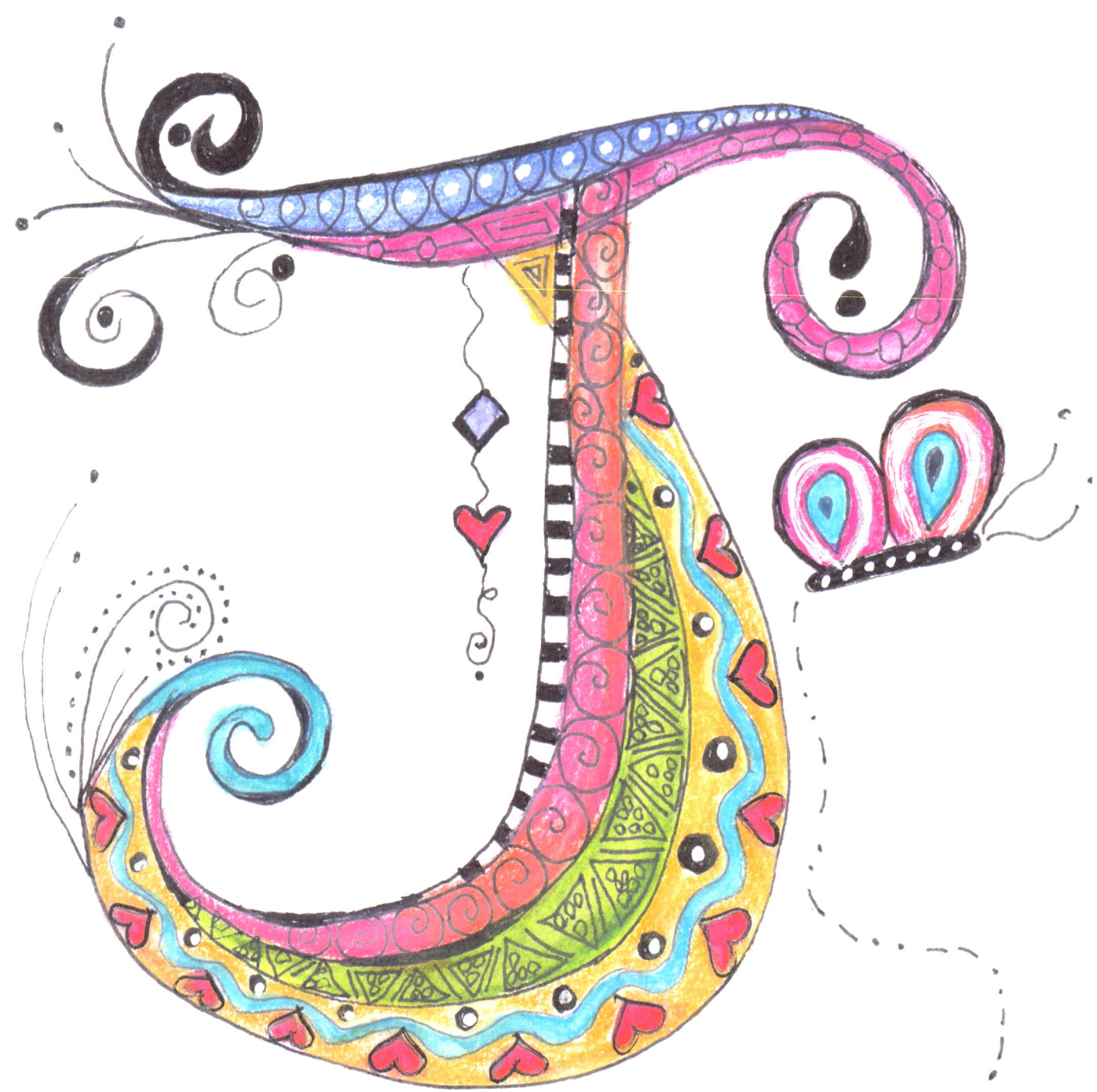

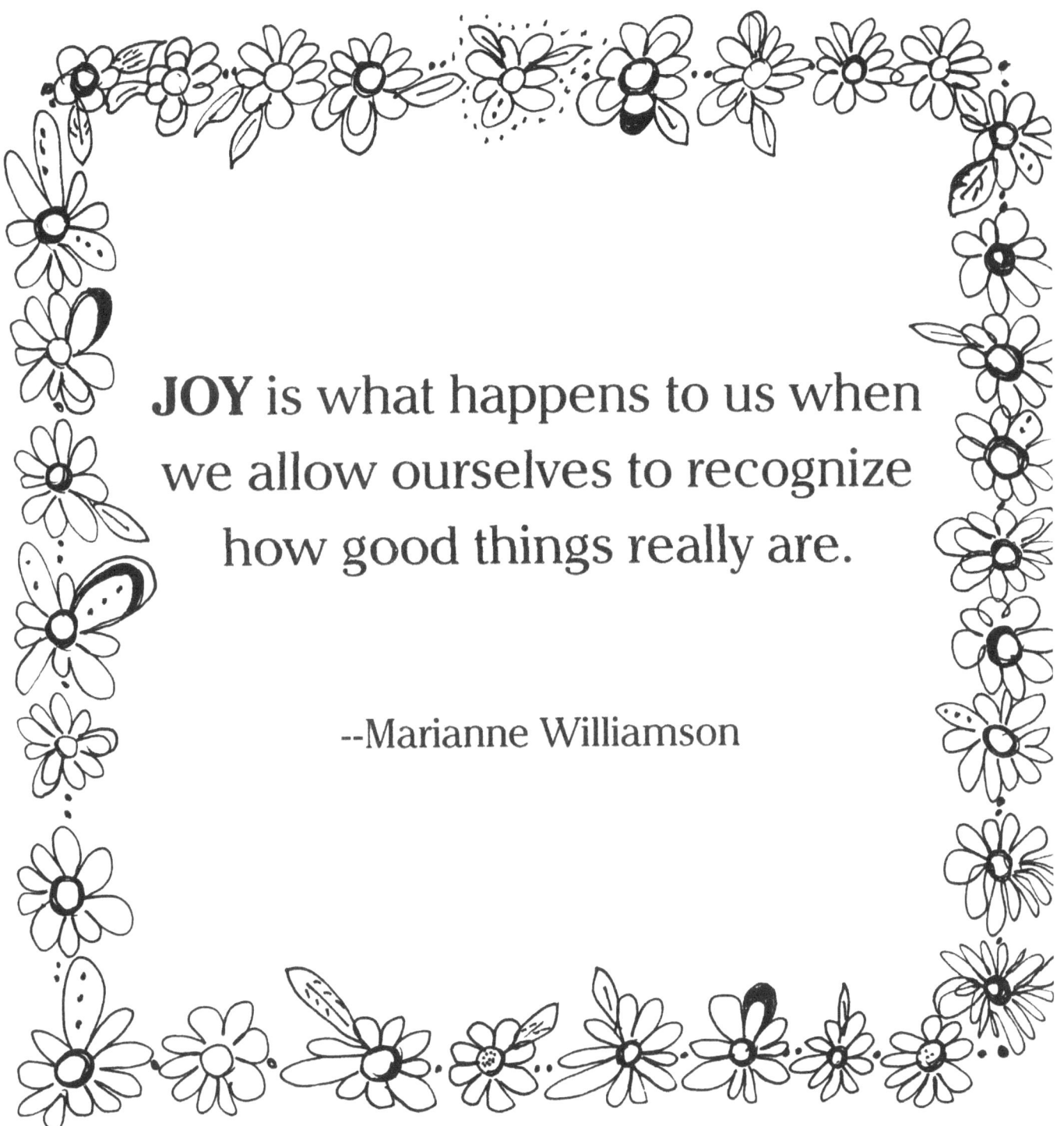

JOY is what happens to us when we allow ourselves to recognize how good things really are.

--Marianne Williamson

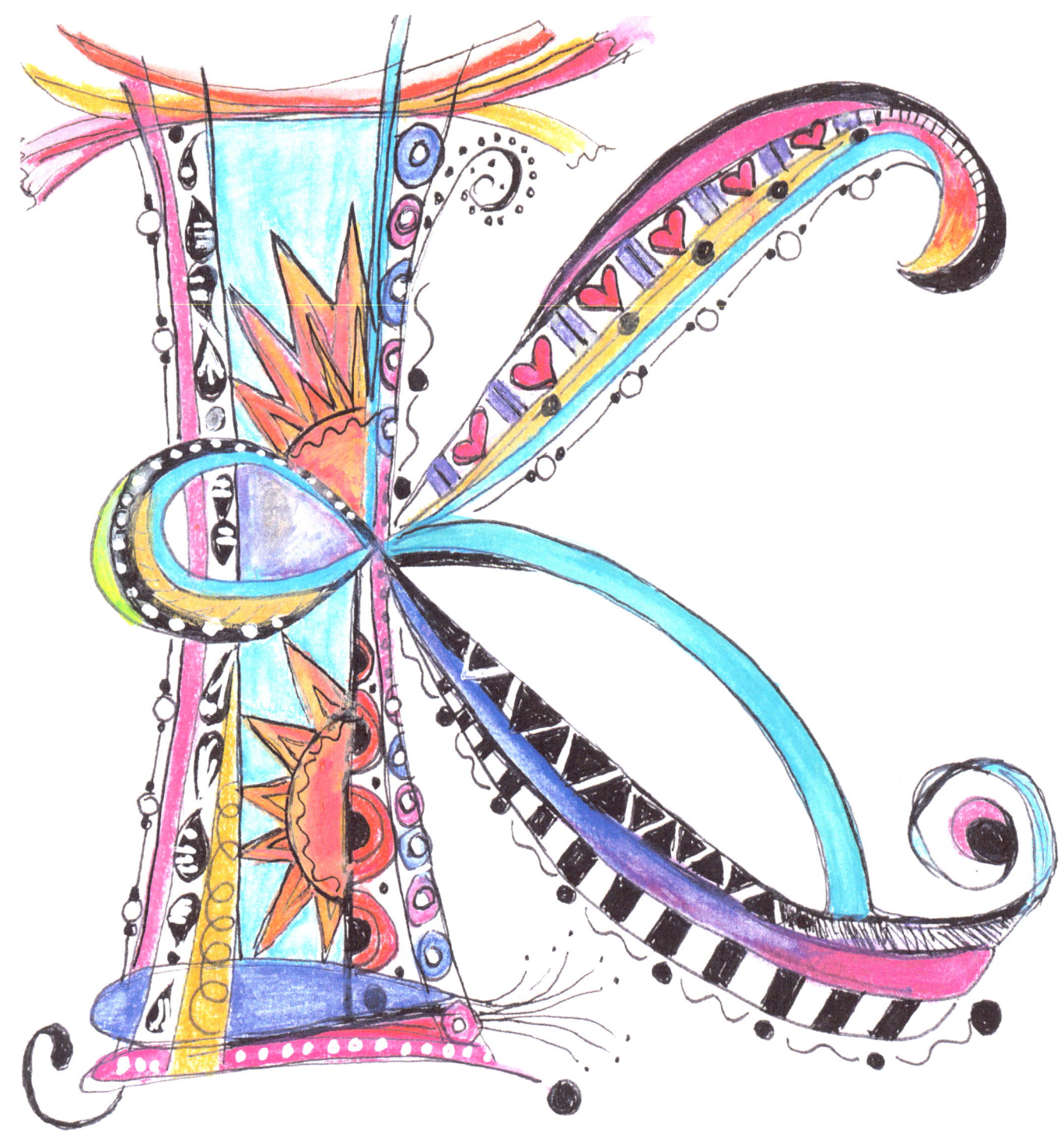

They know me in a way
that no one ever has
They open me to
things I never
knew existed.
They drive me to insanity
and push me to my depths
They are the beat of my heart,
the pulse in my veins,
and the energy in my soul
They are my KIDS

--Douglas Adams

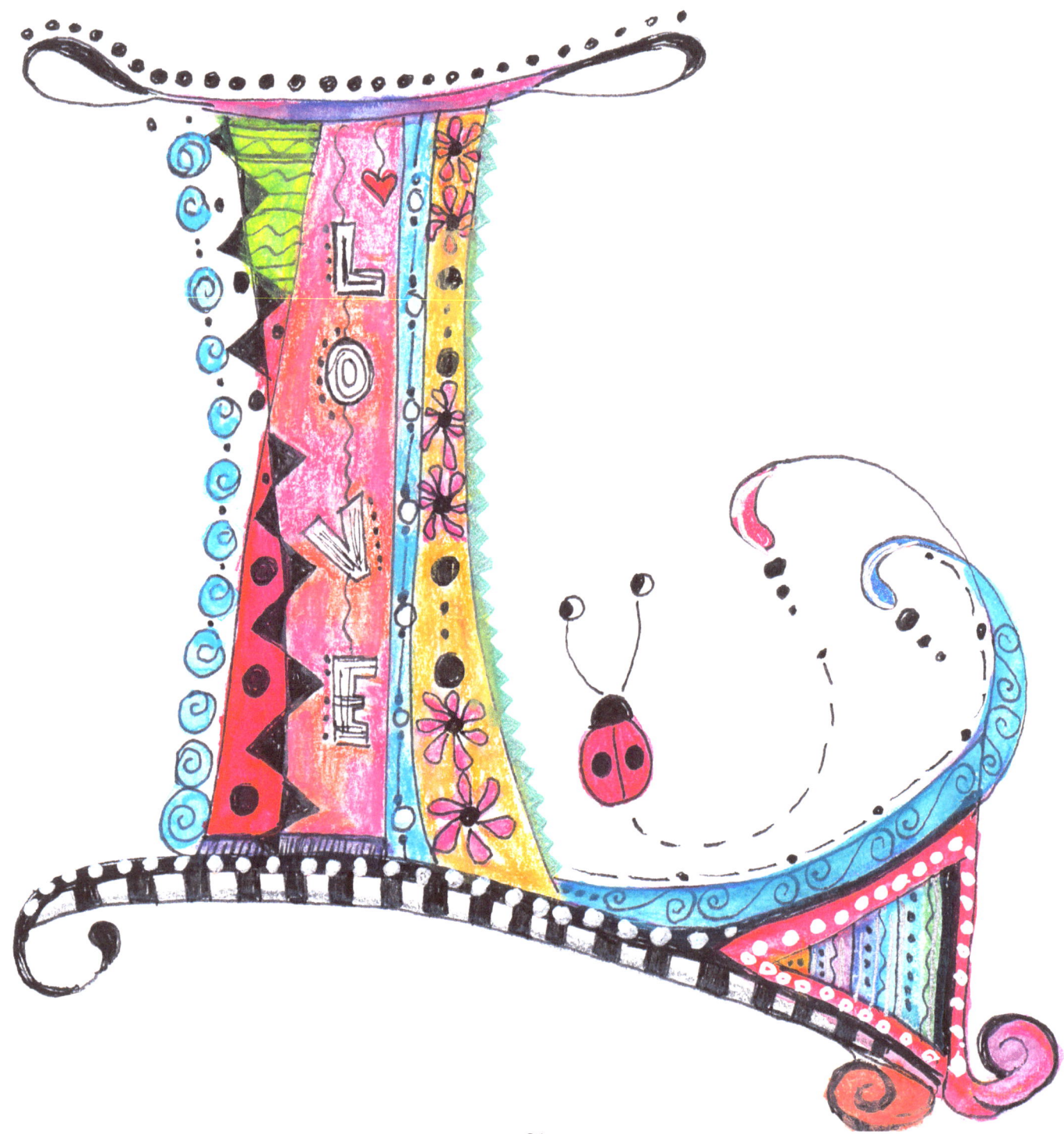

I love people who make me laugh. I honestly think it's the thing I like most, to **LAUGH**. It cures a multitude of ills. It's probably the most important thing in a person.

--Audrey Hepburn

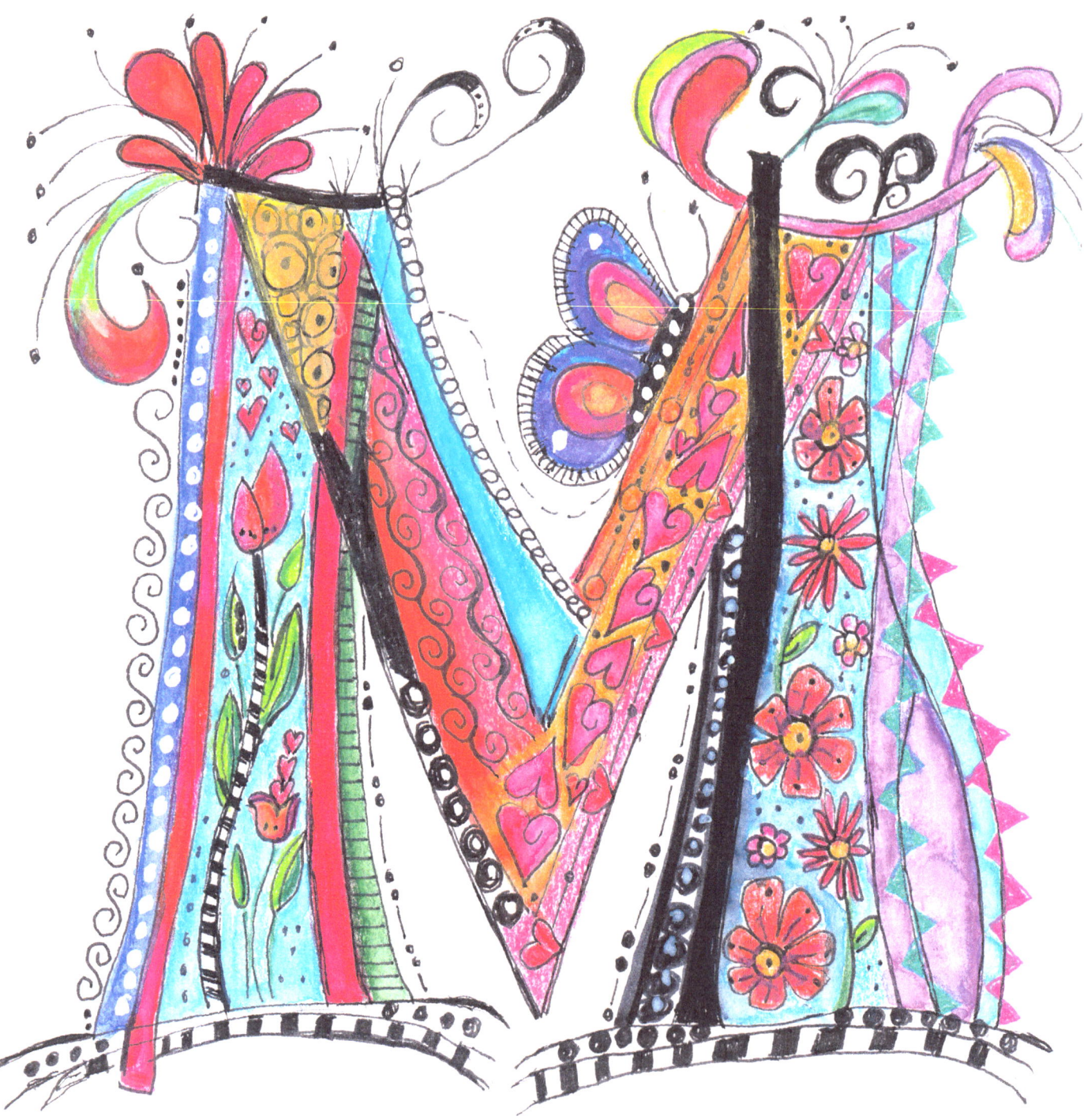

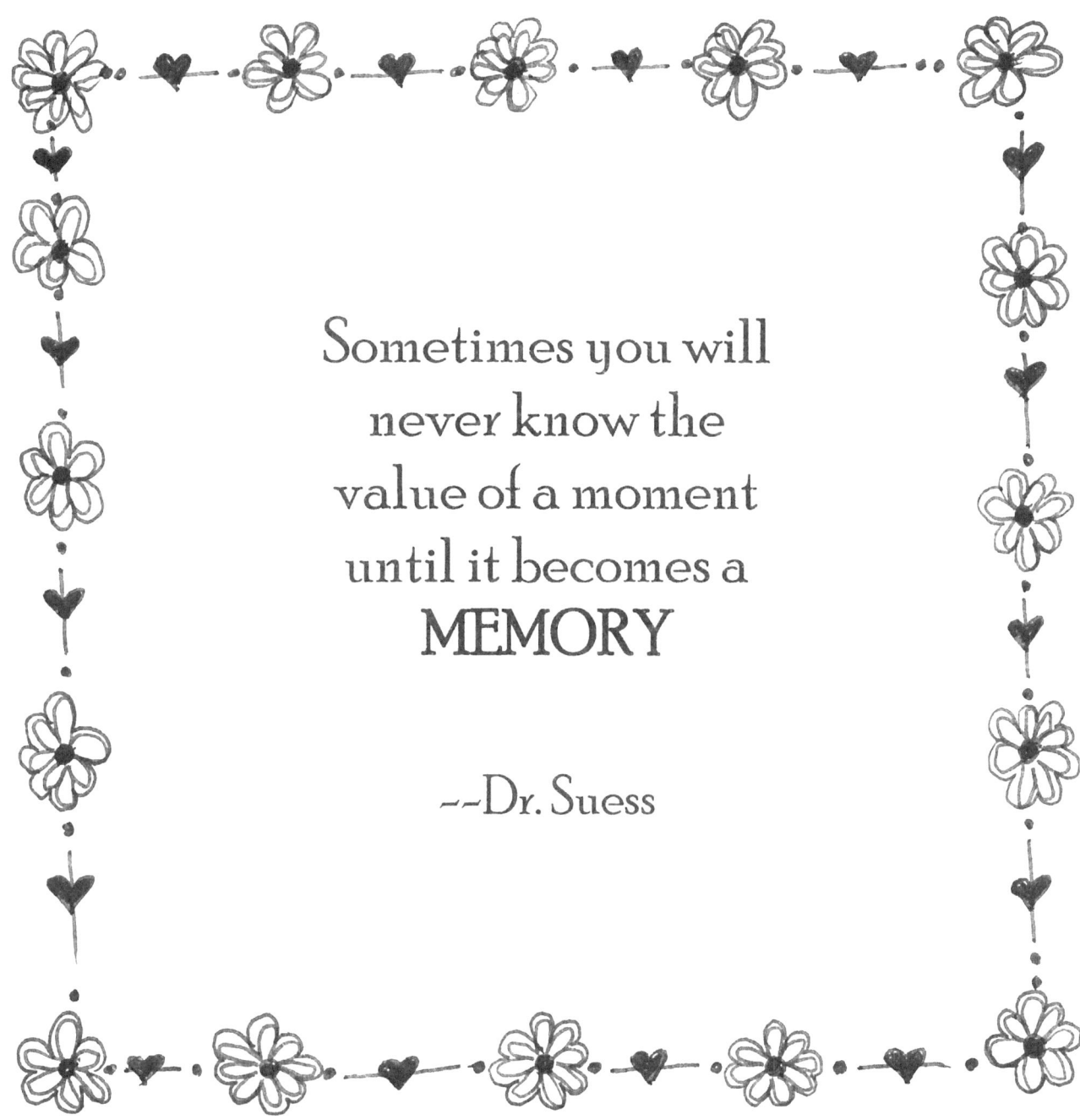

Sometimes you will
never know the
value of a moment
until it becomes a
MEMORY

--Dr. Suess

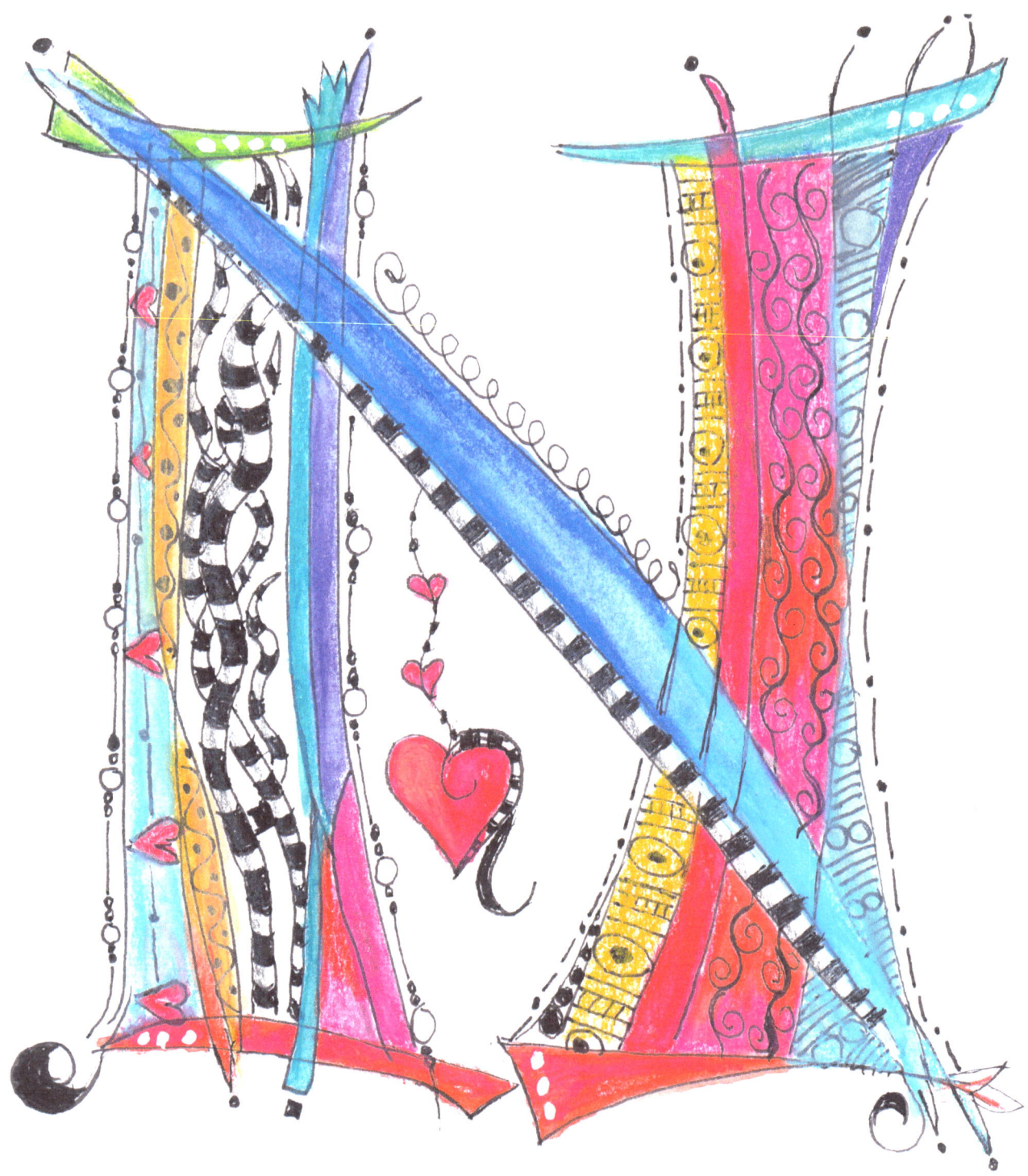

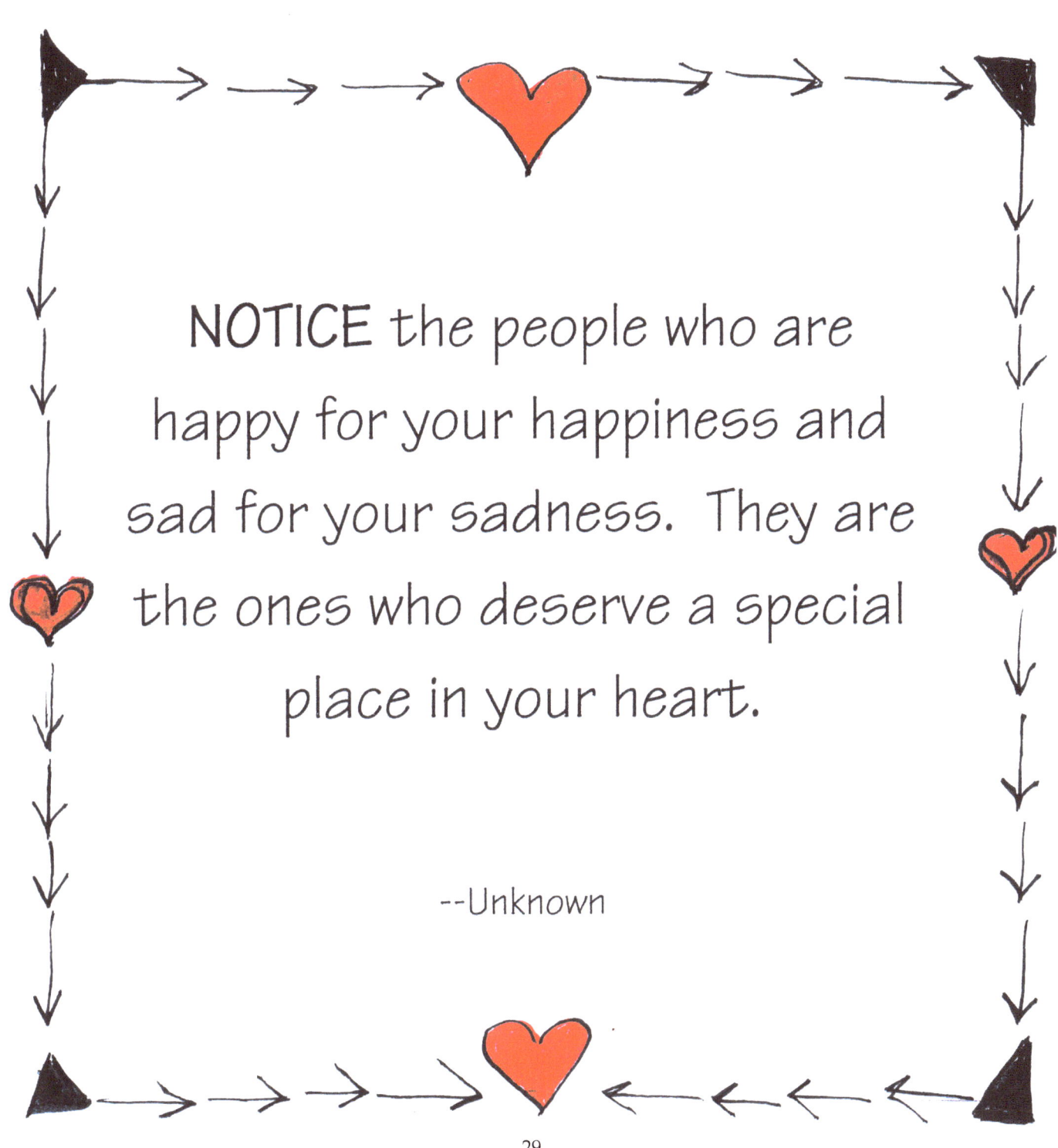

NOTICE the people who are happy for your happiness and sad for your sadness. They are the ones who deserve a special place in your heart.

--Unknown

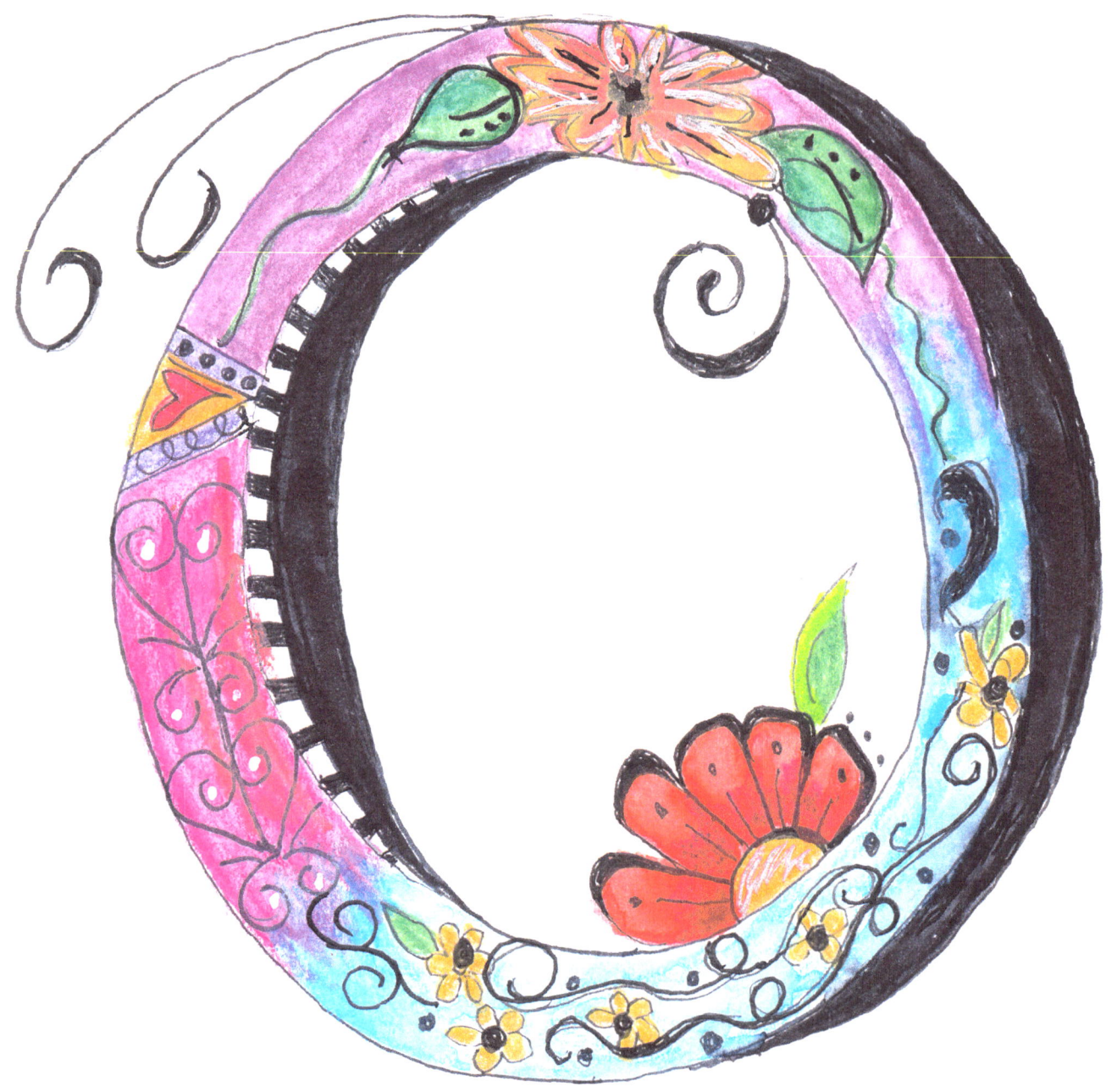

OLD enough to know better.

Young enough to do it anyway.

--Unknown

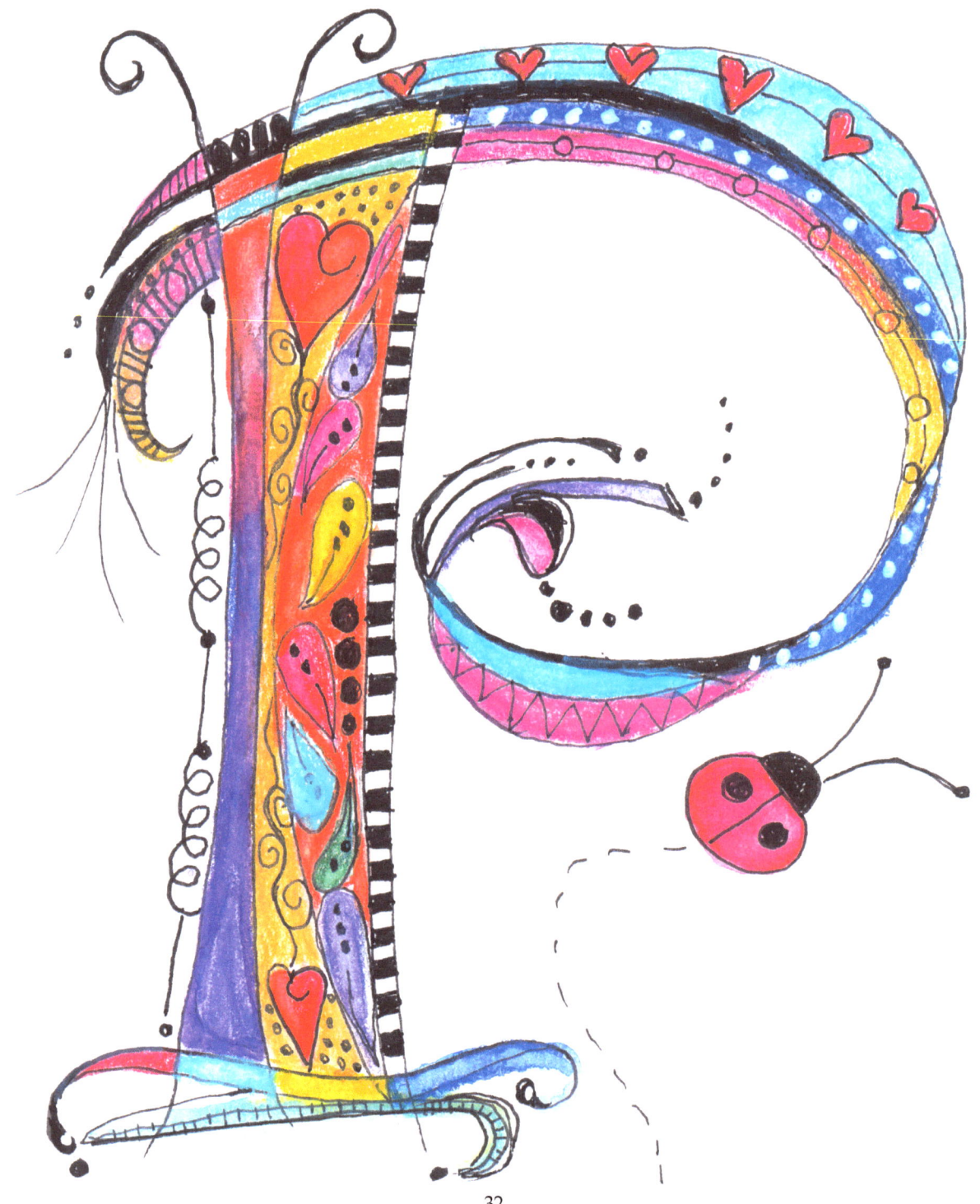

32

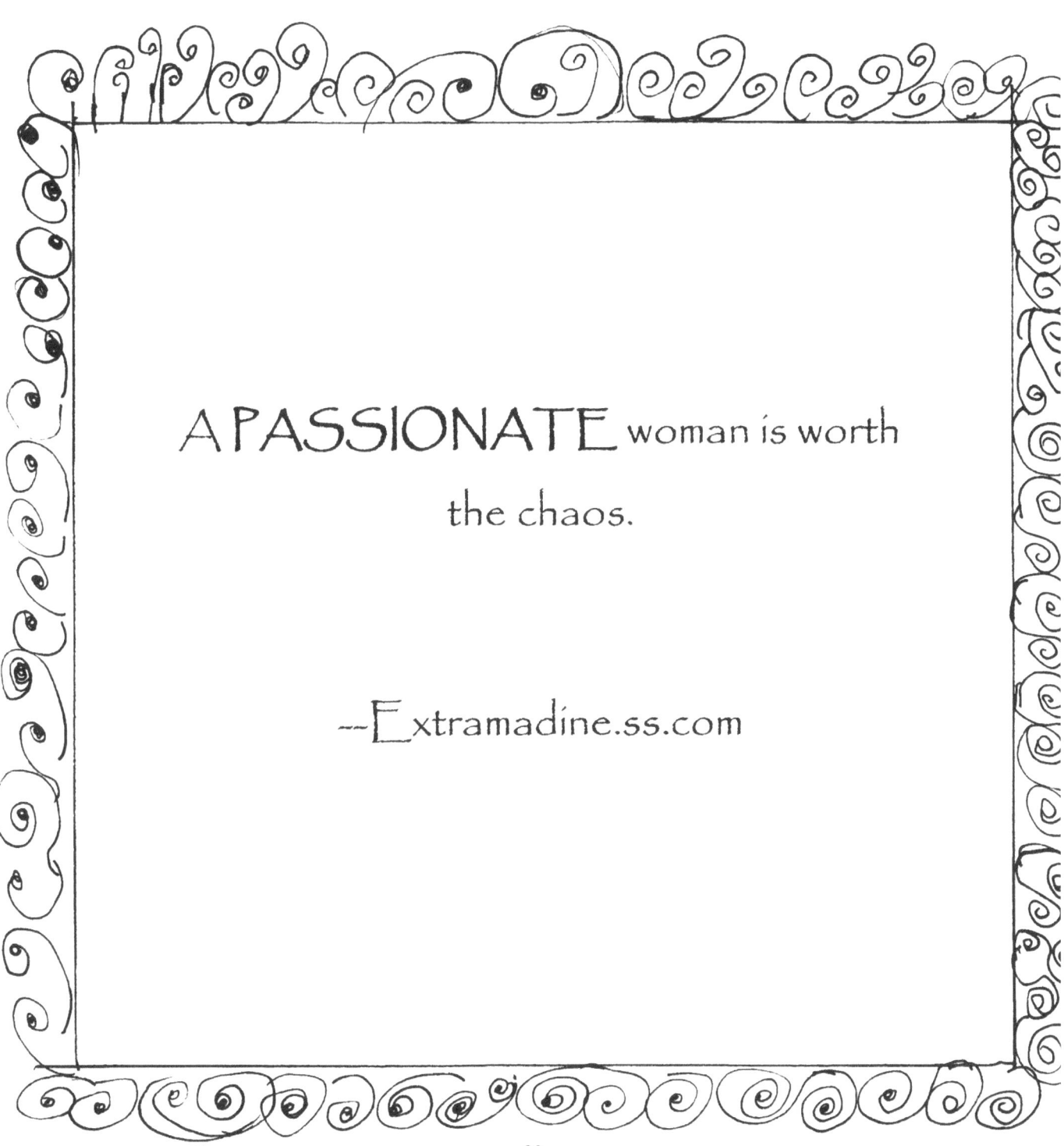

A PASSIONATE woman is worth

the chaos.

--Extramadine.ss.com

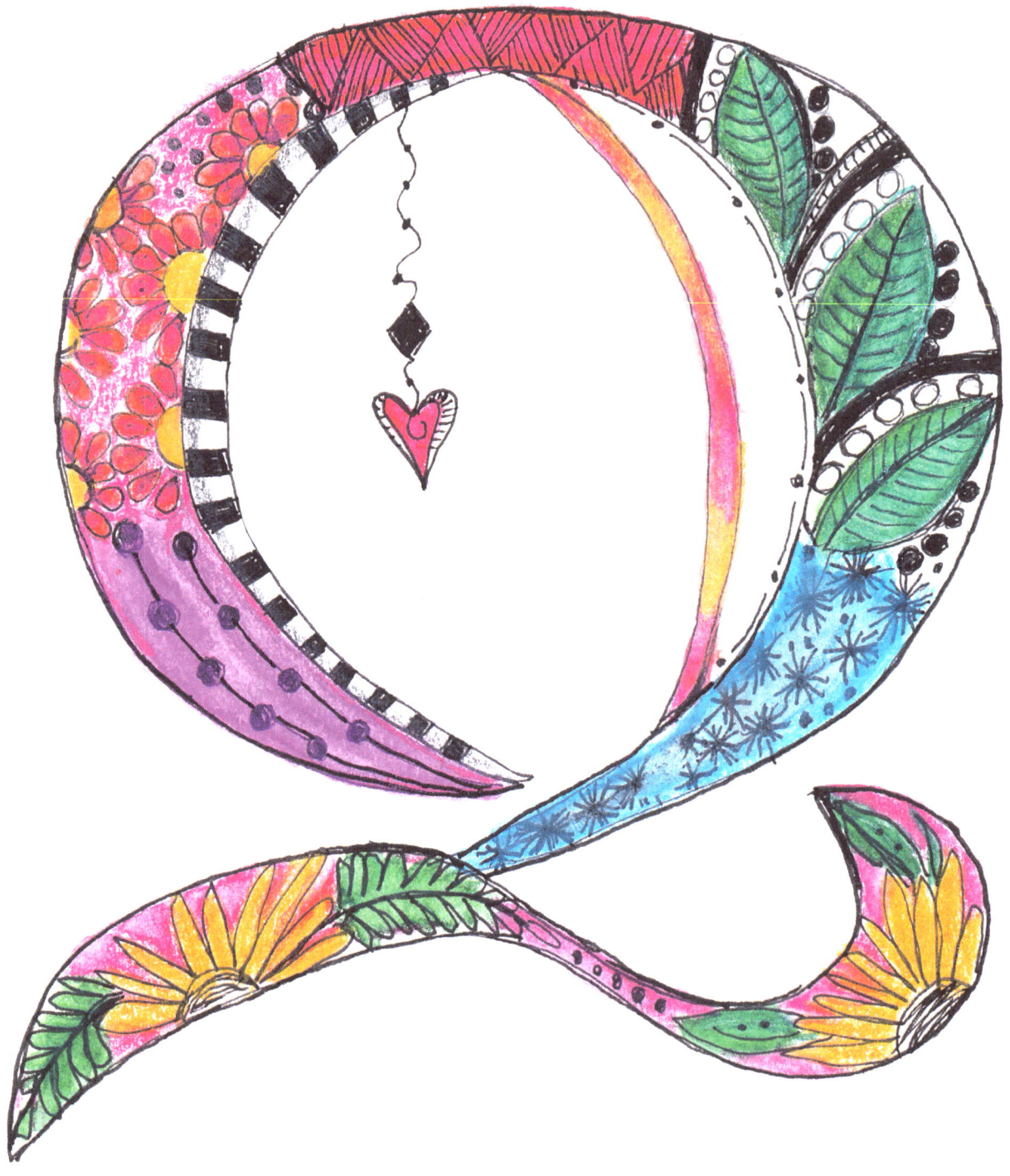

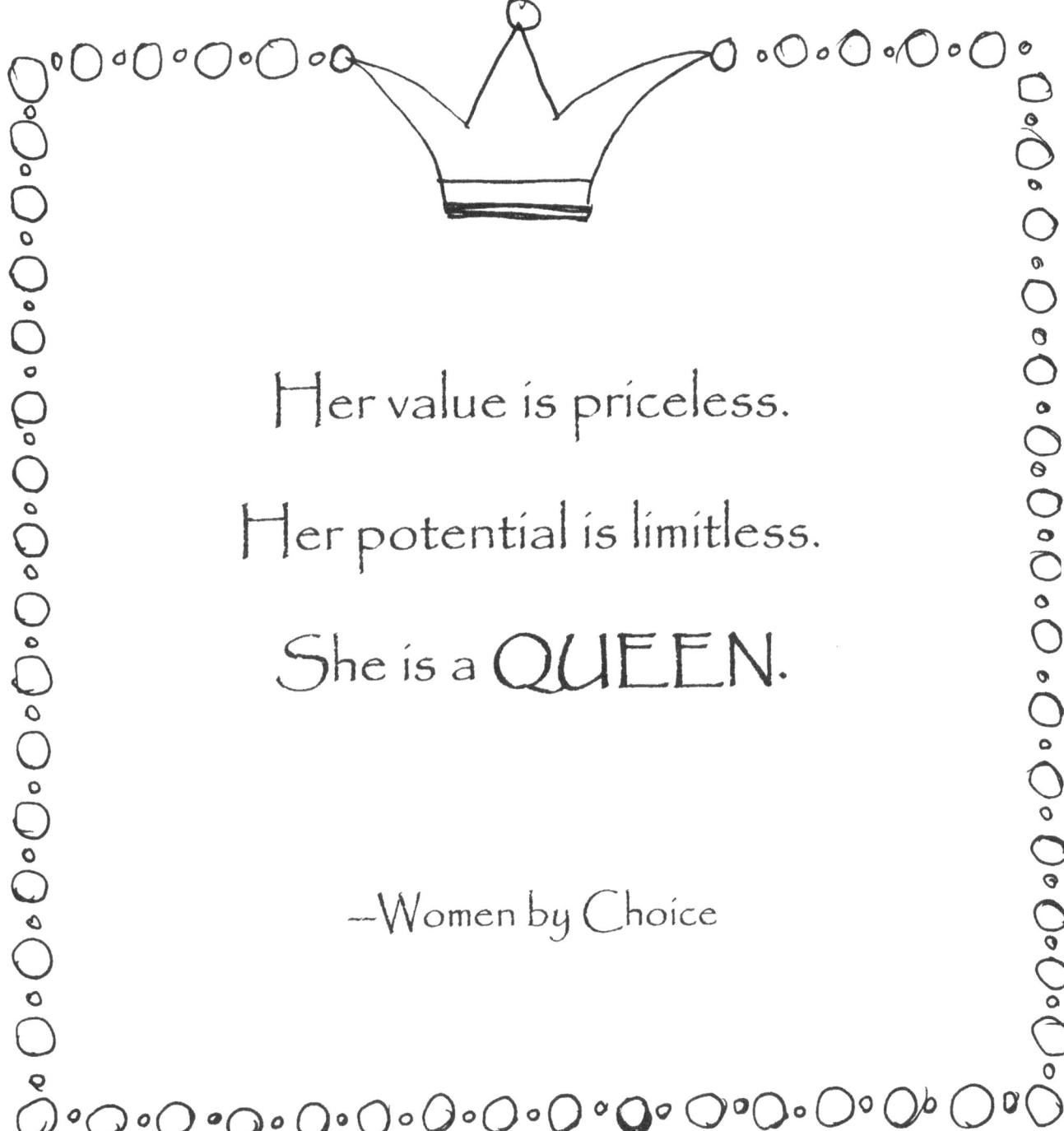

Her value is priceless.

Her potential is limitless.

She is a QUEEN.

—Women by Choice

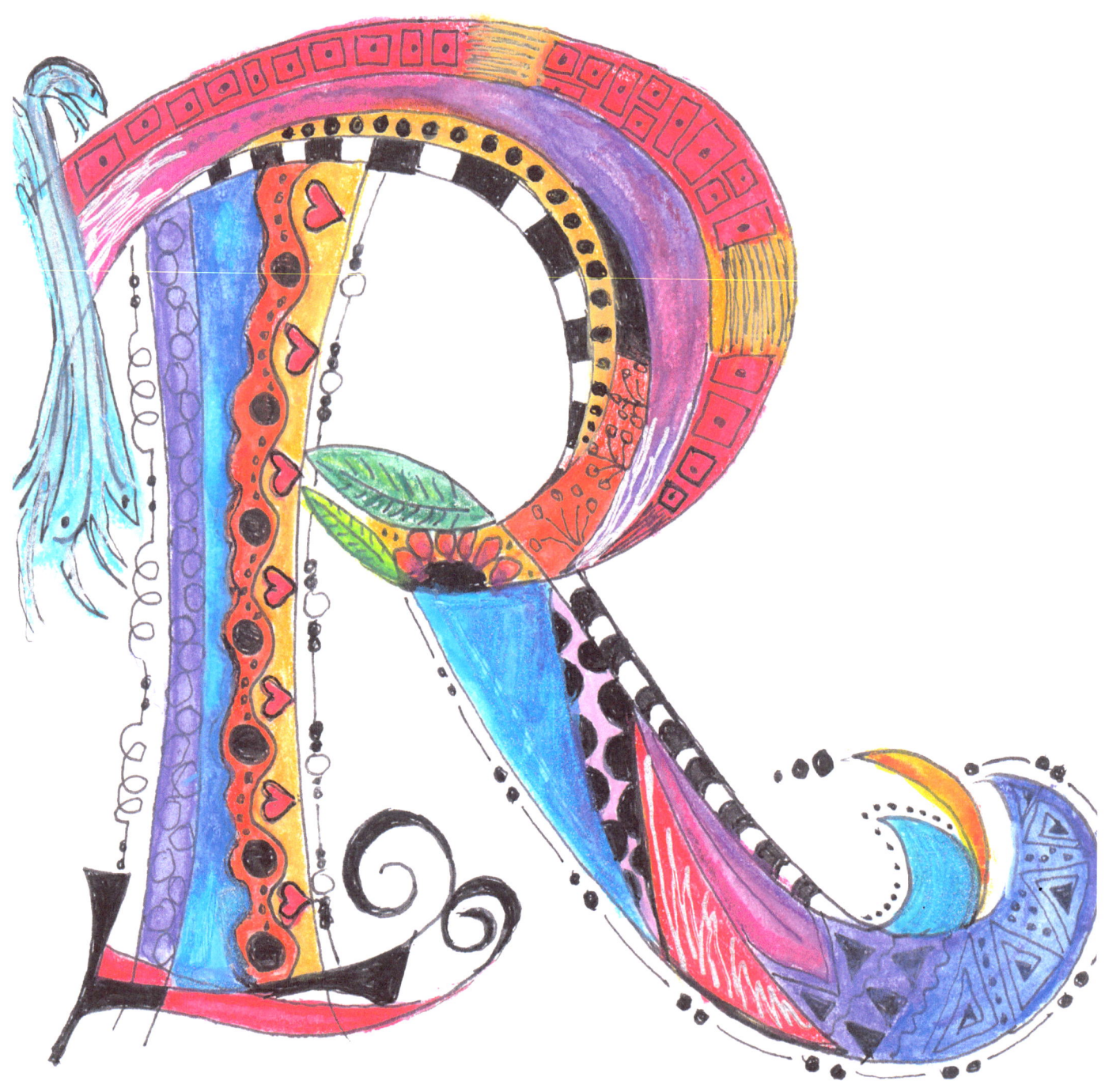

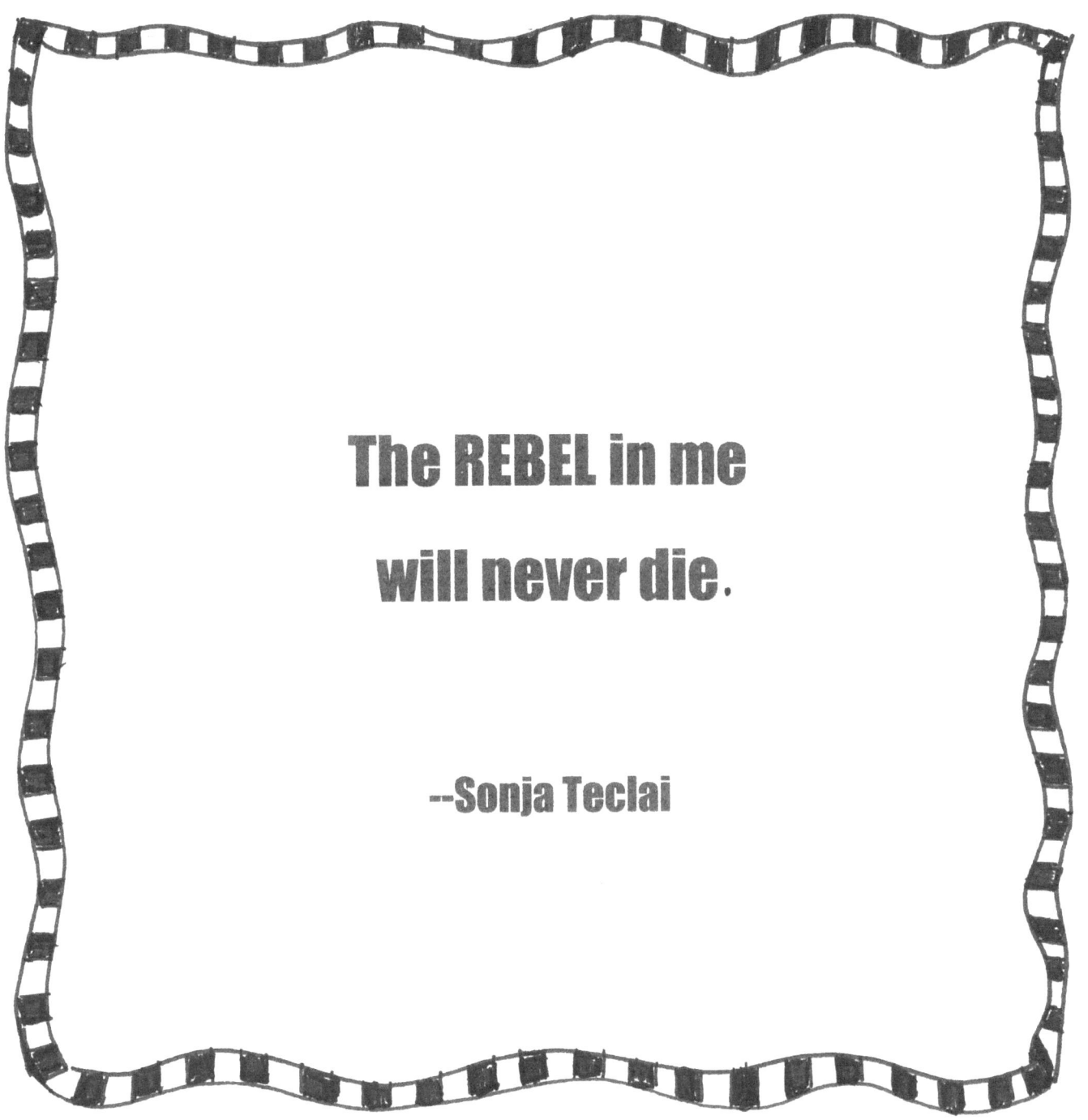

The REBEL in me

will never die.

--Sonja Teclai

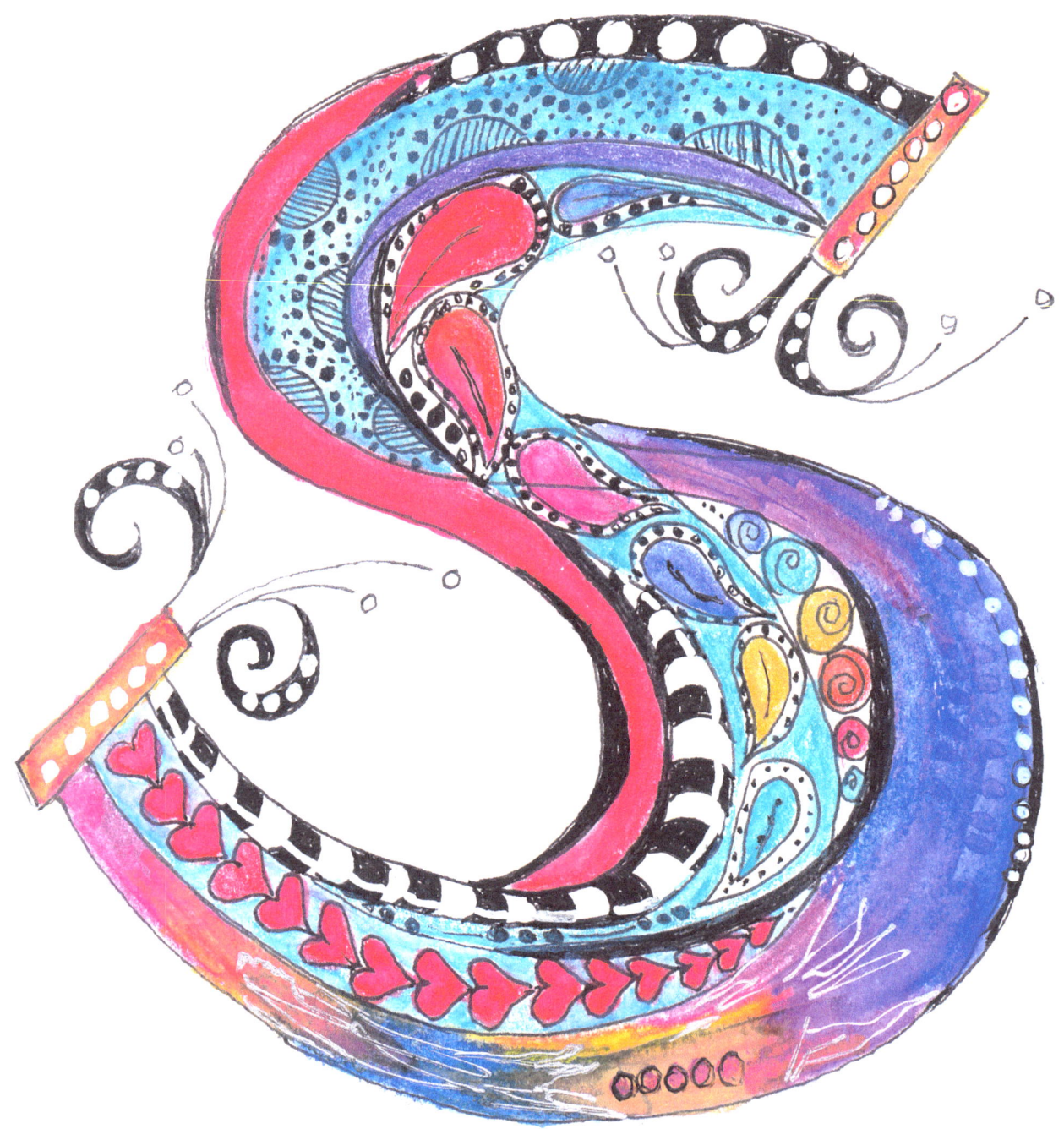

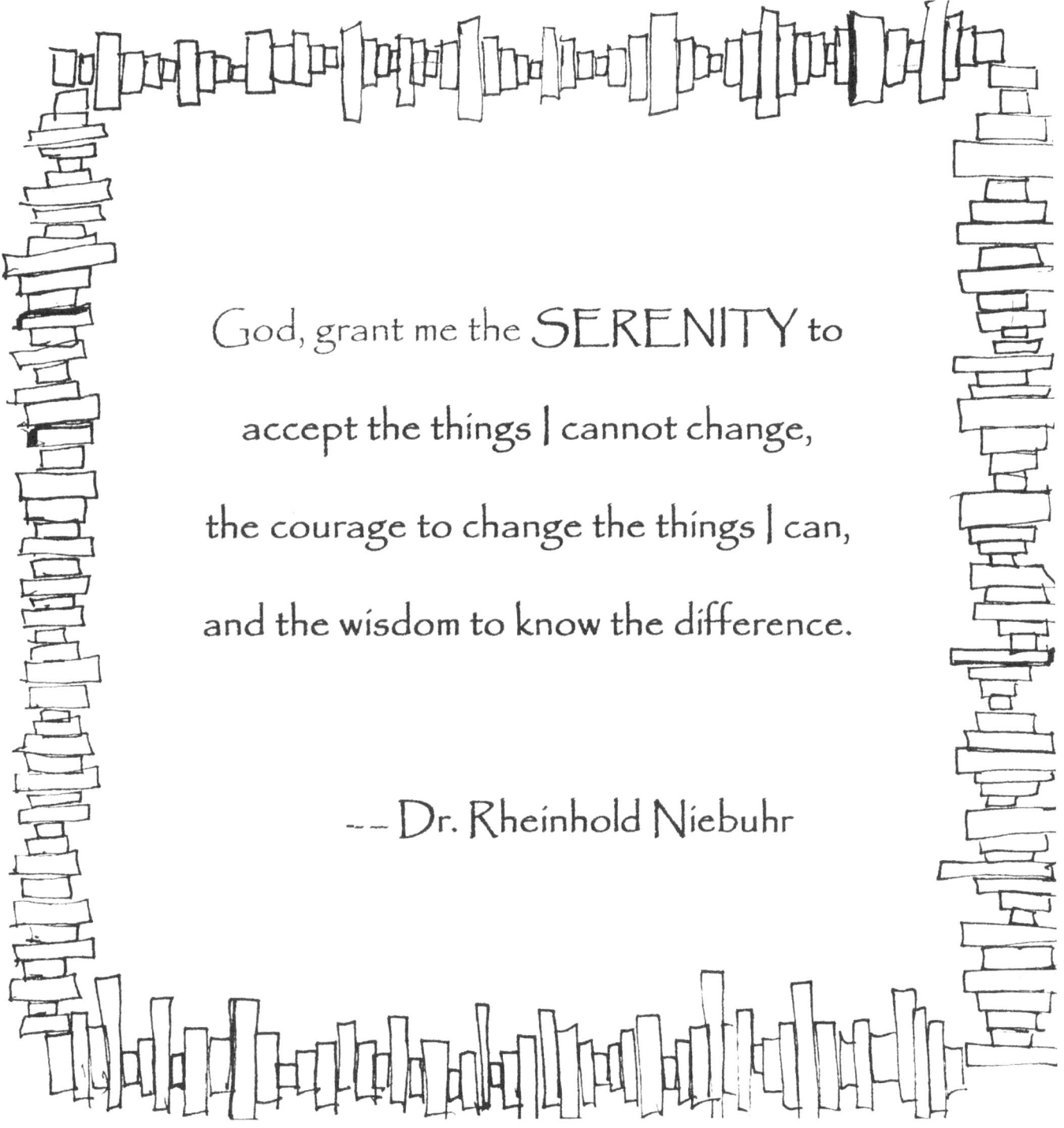

God, grant me the SERENITY to

accept the things I cannot change,

the courage to change the things I can,

and the wisdom to know the difference.

--- Dr. Rheinhold Niebuhr

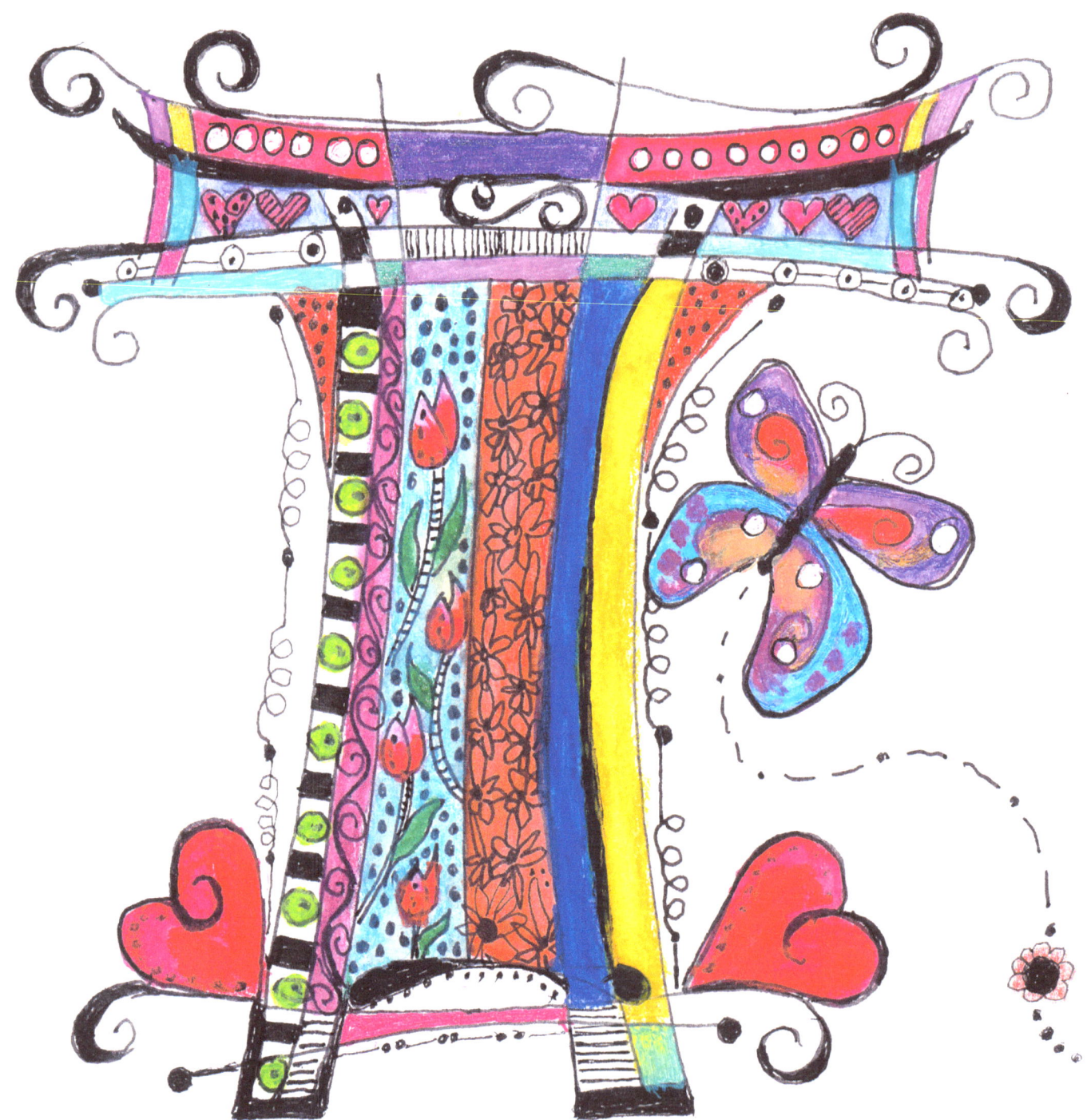

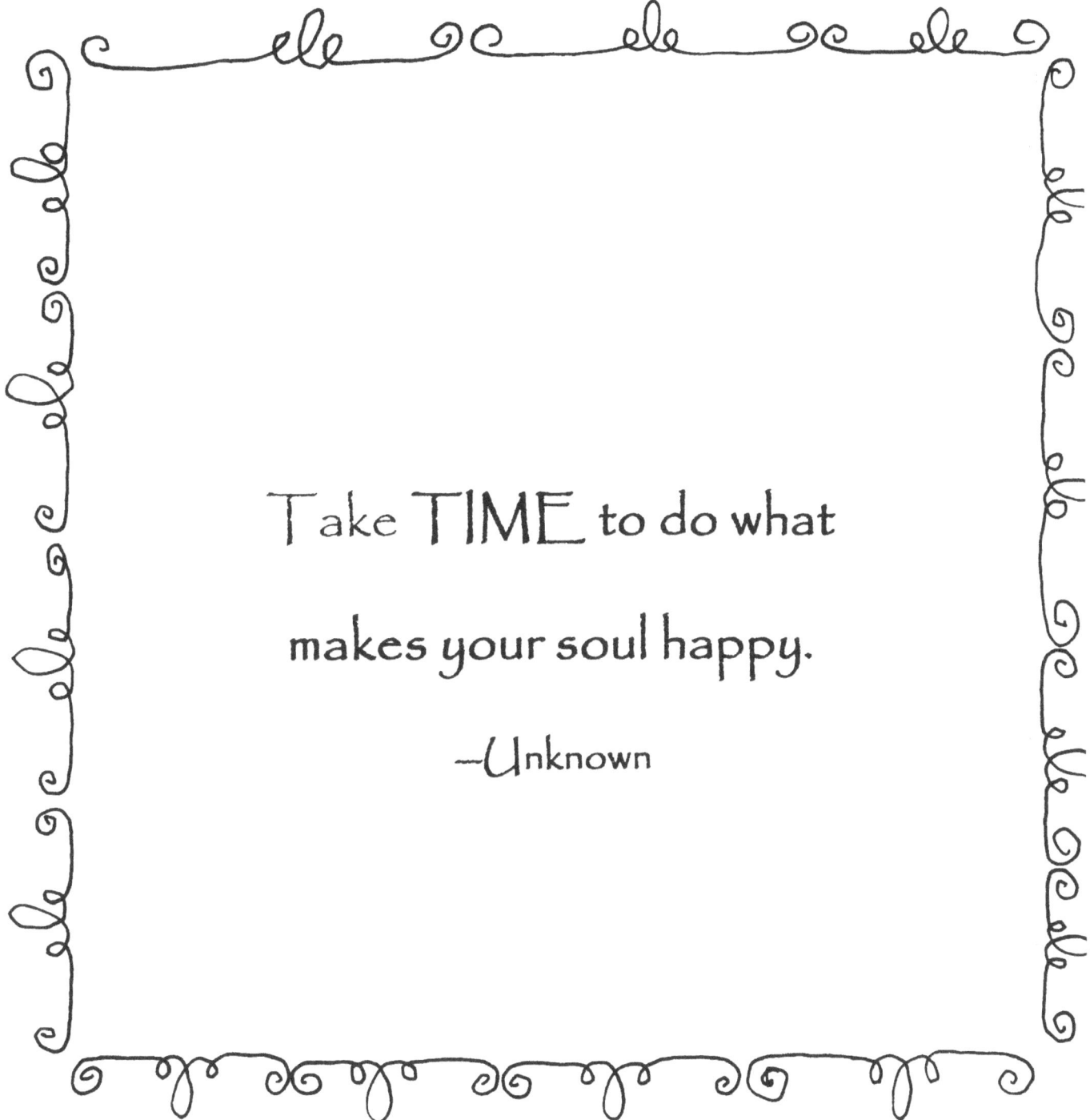

Take TIME to do what

makes your soul happy.

—Unknown

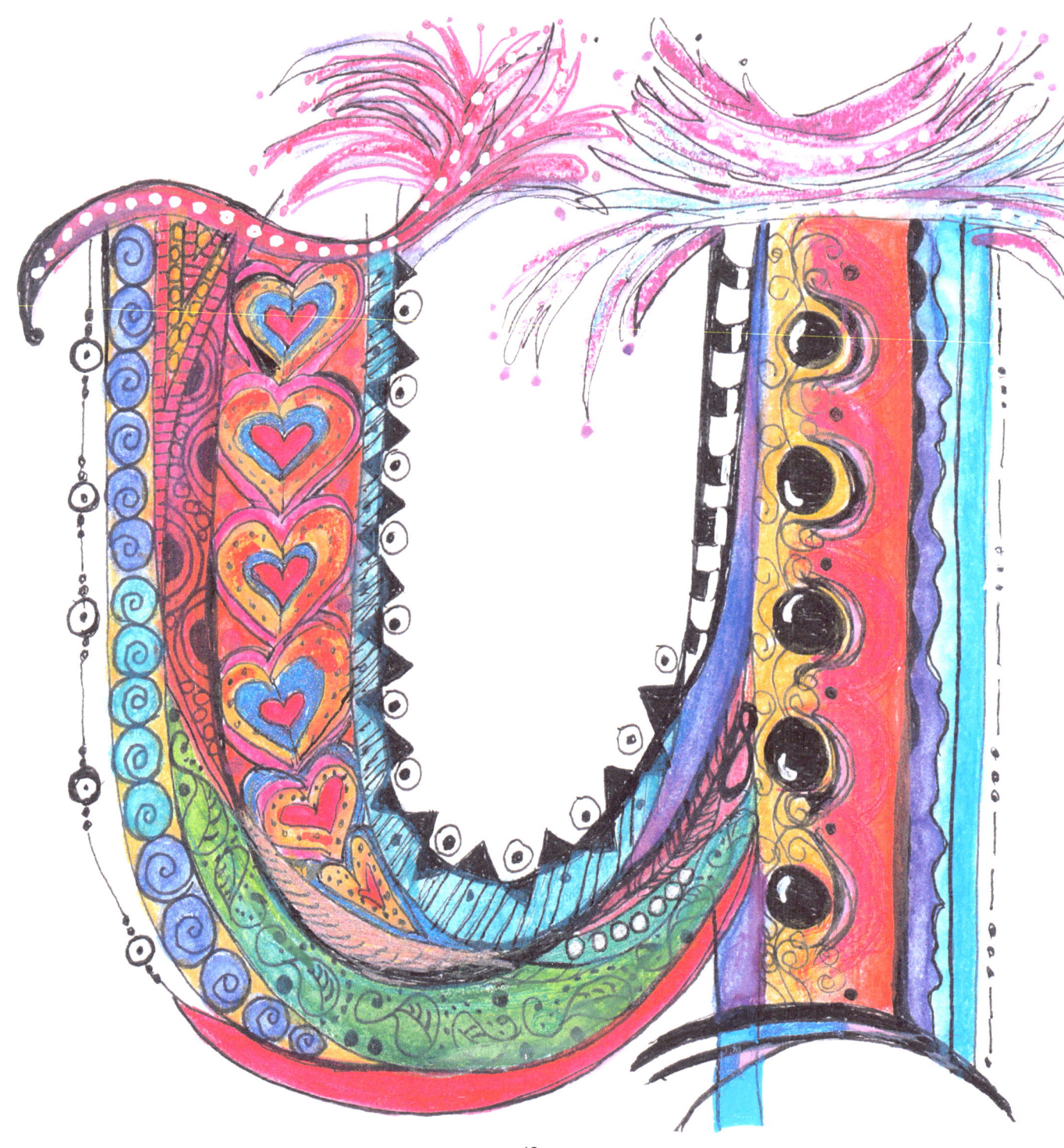

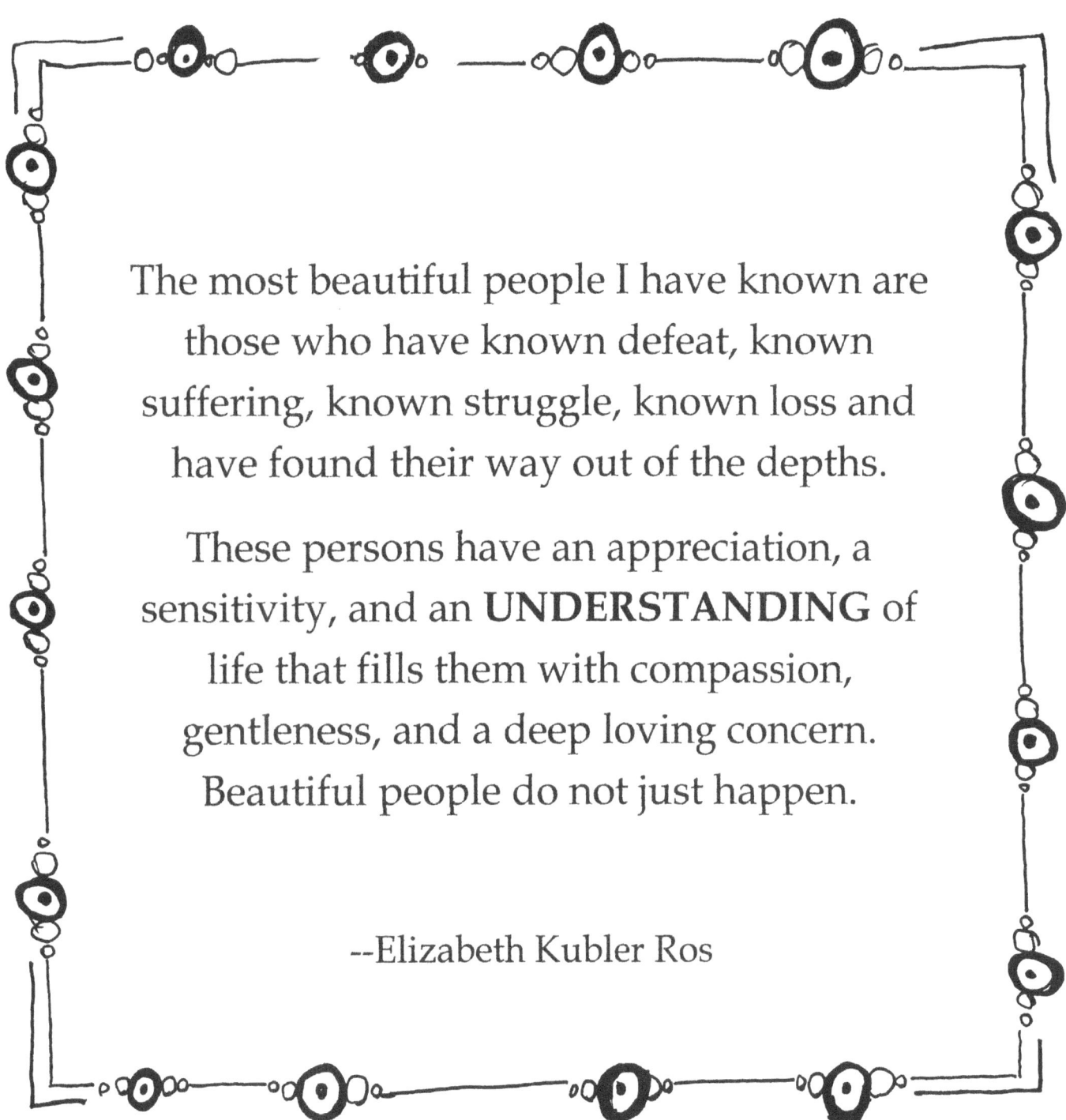

The most beautiful people I have known are those who have known defeat, known suffering, known struggle, known loss and have found their way out of the depths.

These persons have an appreciation, a sensitivity, and an **UNDERSTANDING** of life that fills them with compassion, gentleness, and a deep loving concern. Beautiful people do not just happen.

--Elizabeth Kubler Ros

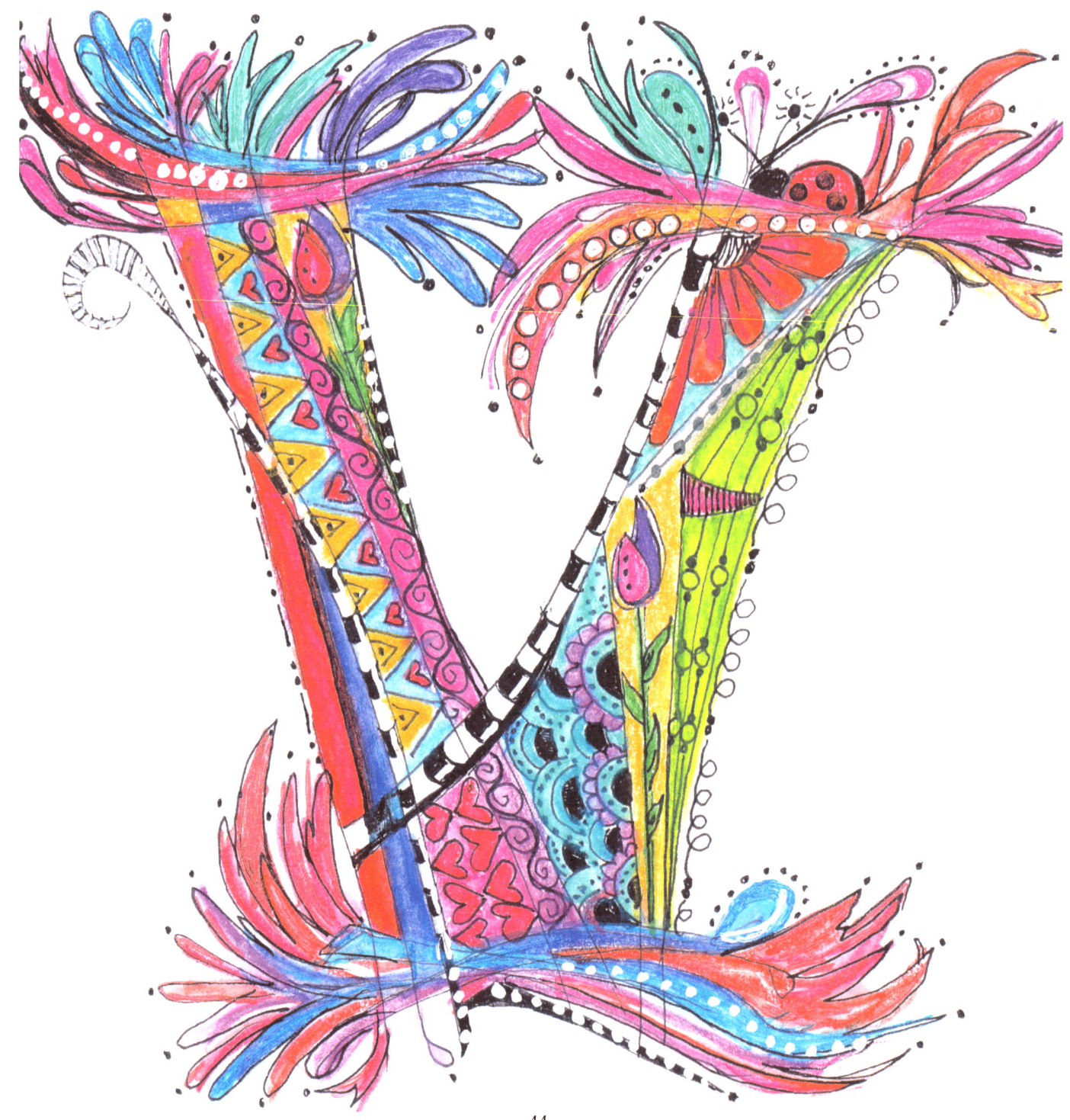

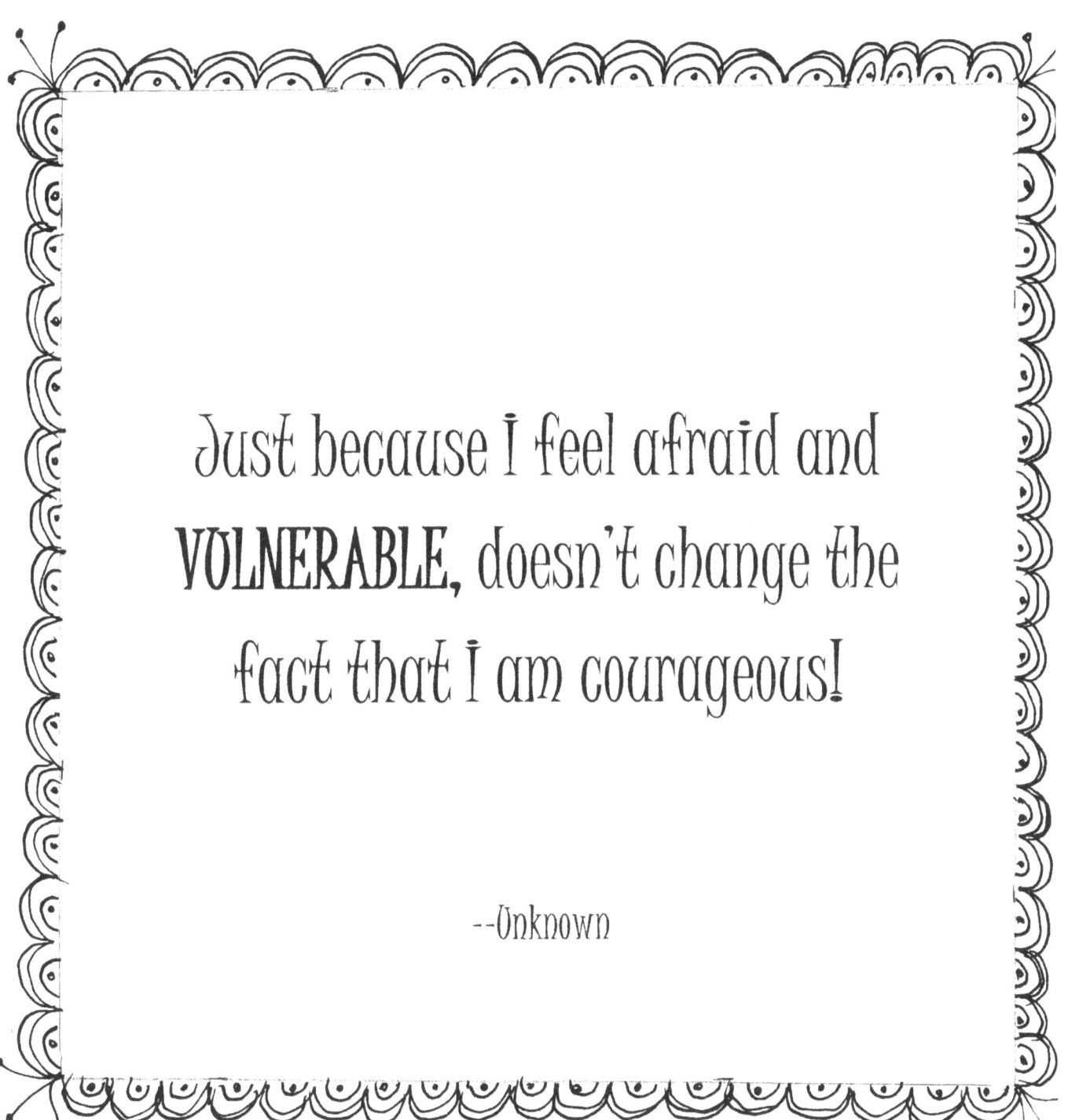

Just because I feel afraid and **VULNERABLE,** doesn't change the fact that I am courageous!

--Unknown

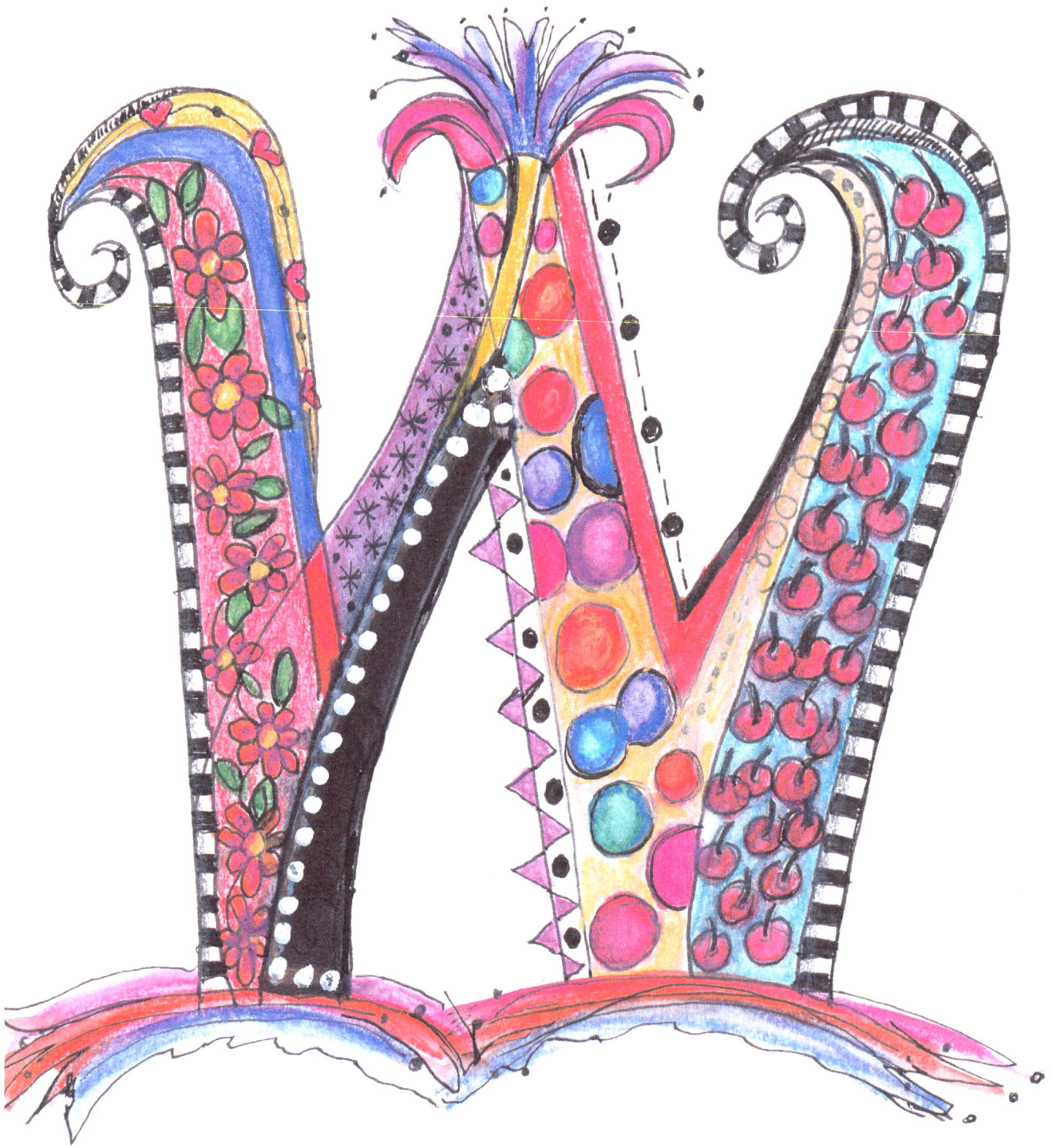

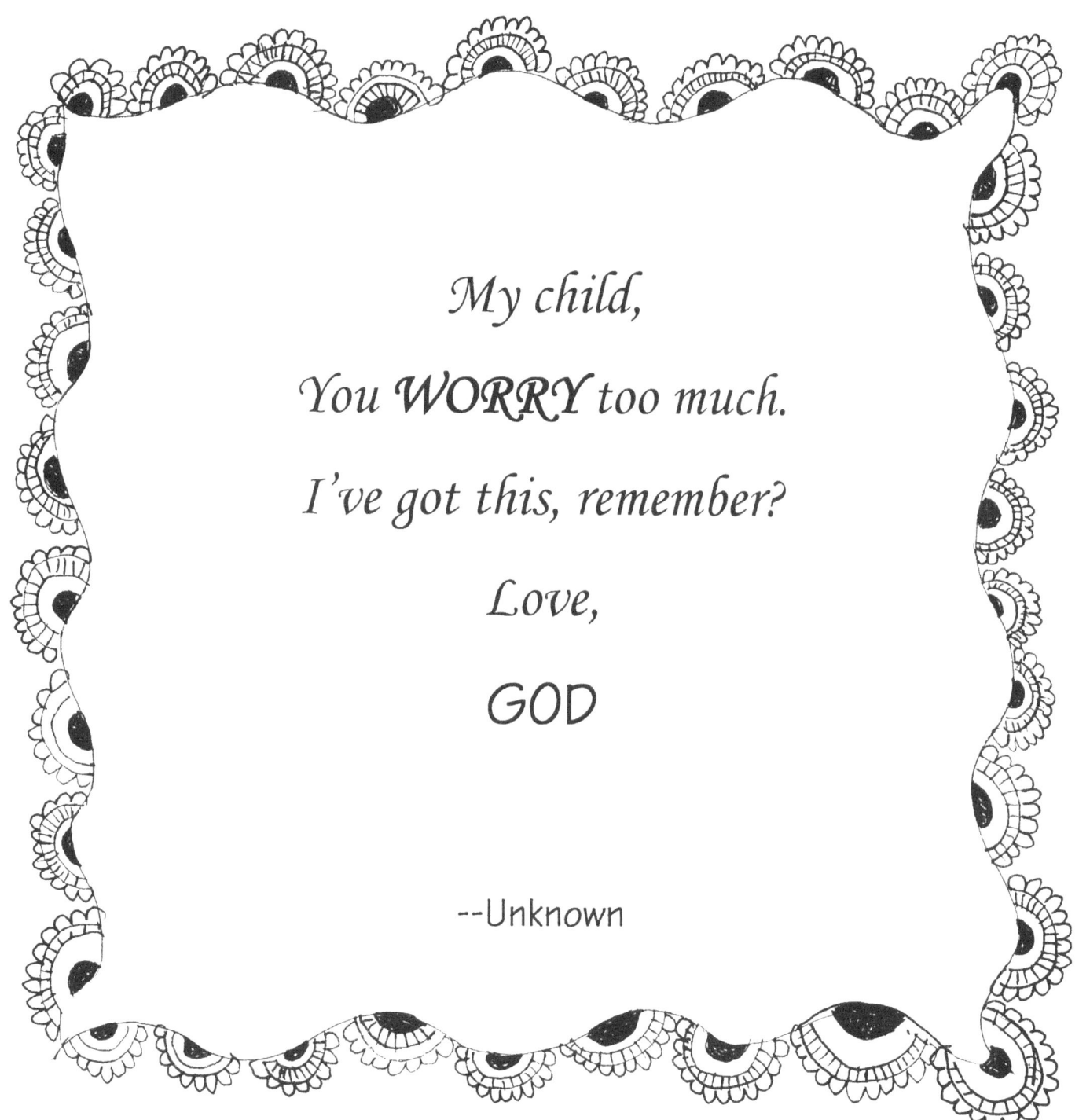

My child,

*You **WORRY** too much.*

I've got this, remember?

Love,

GOD

--Unknown

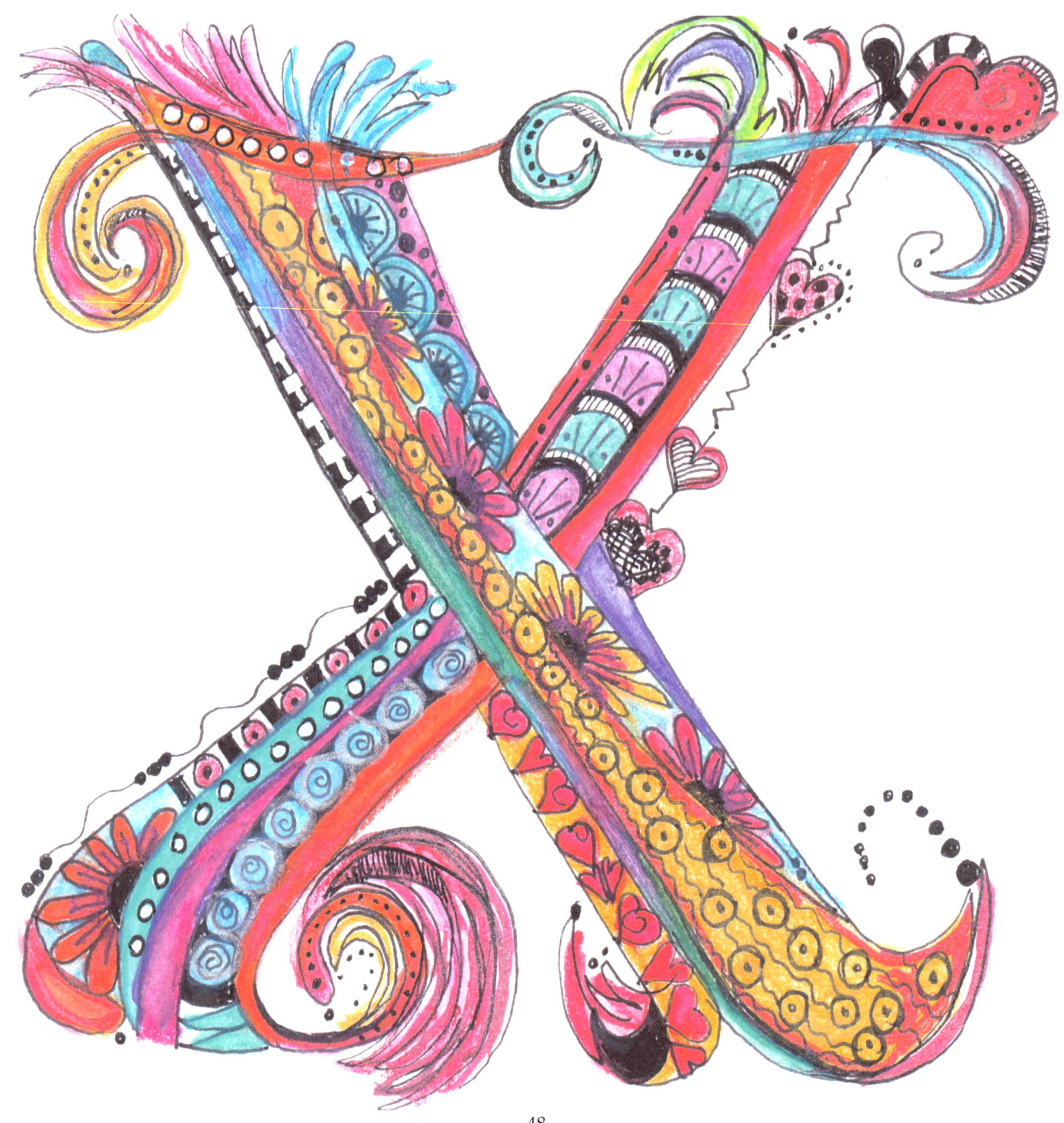

"X" marks the spot. Stand with your heart and soul firmly planted in today. Life is not a dress rehearsal. Yesterday is done. We did the best we could and tomorrow is not yet here. Today is all we are promised. Make the most of it.

--Tiffany Taylor Wright

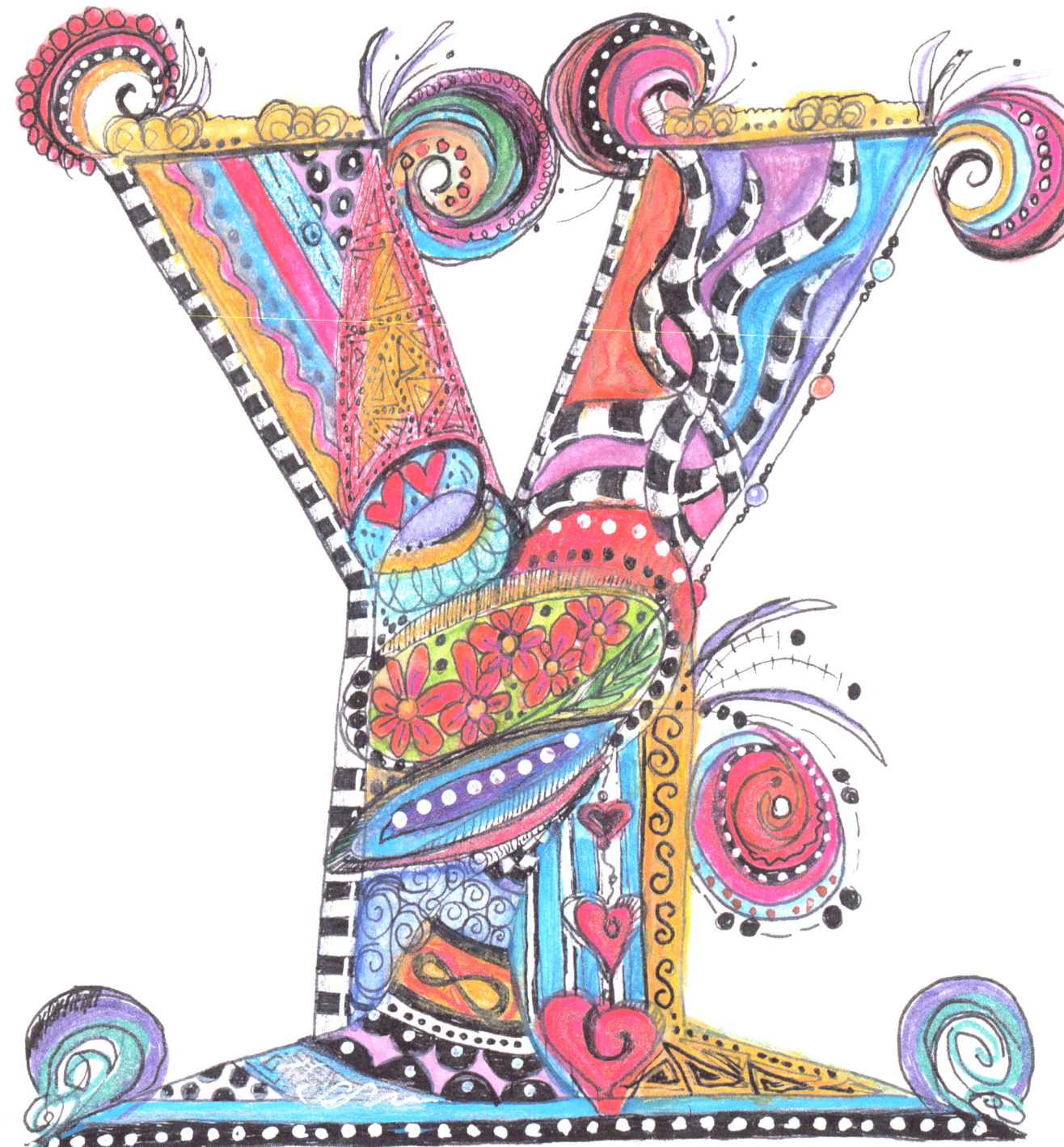

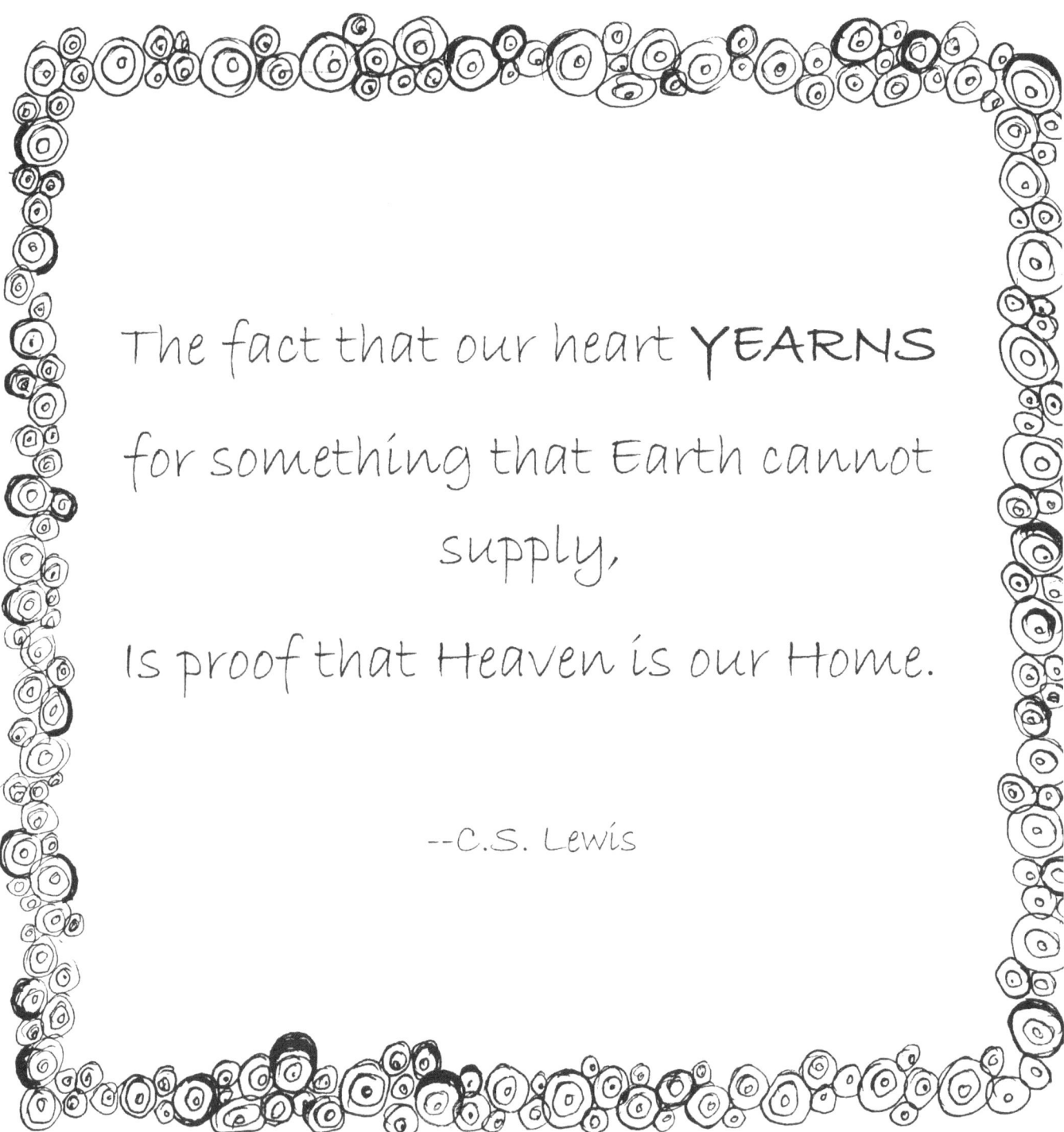

The fact that our heart YEARNS

for something that Earth cannot

supply,

Is proof that Heaven is our Home.

--C.S. Lewis

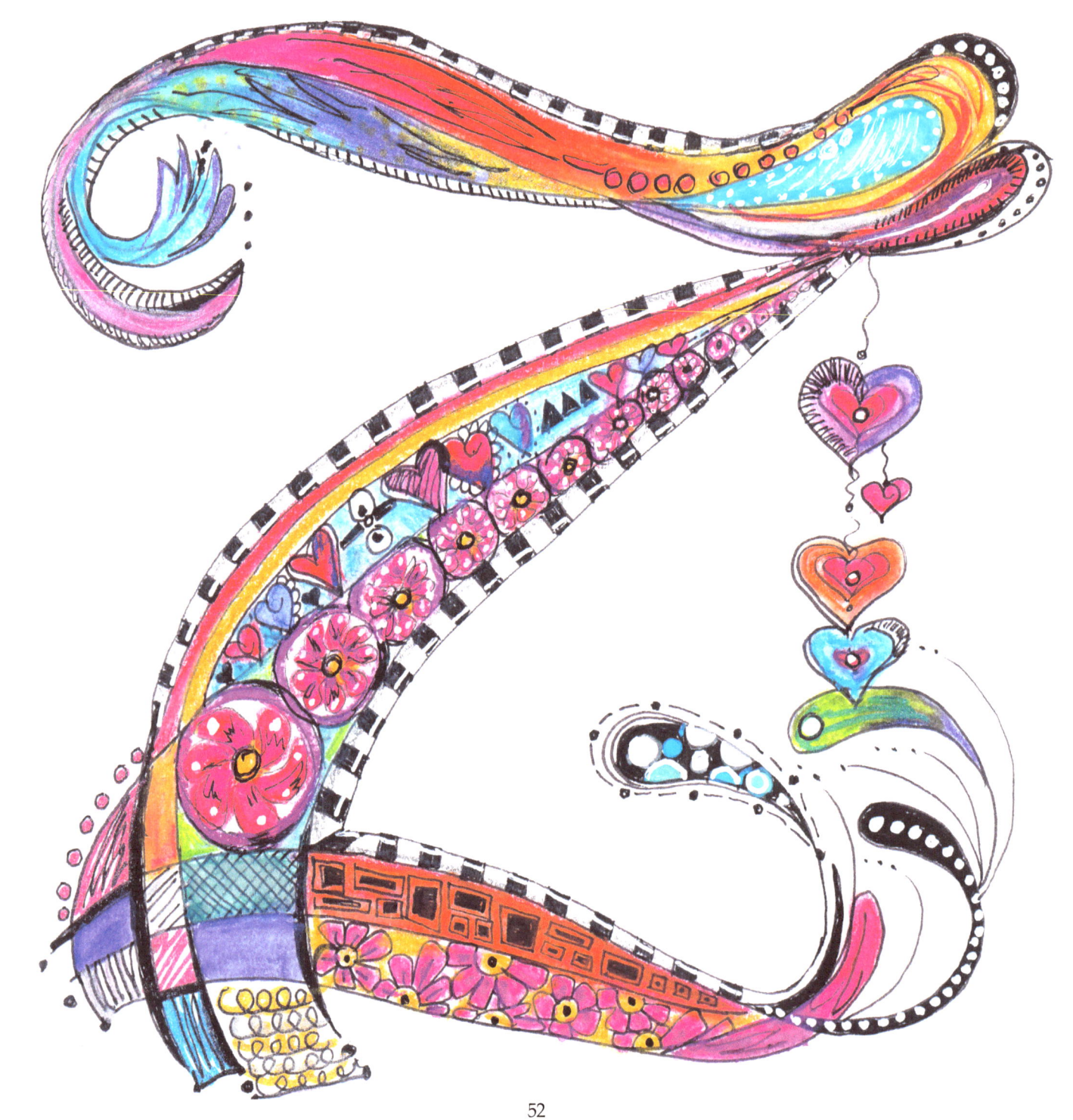

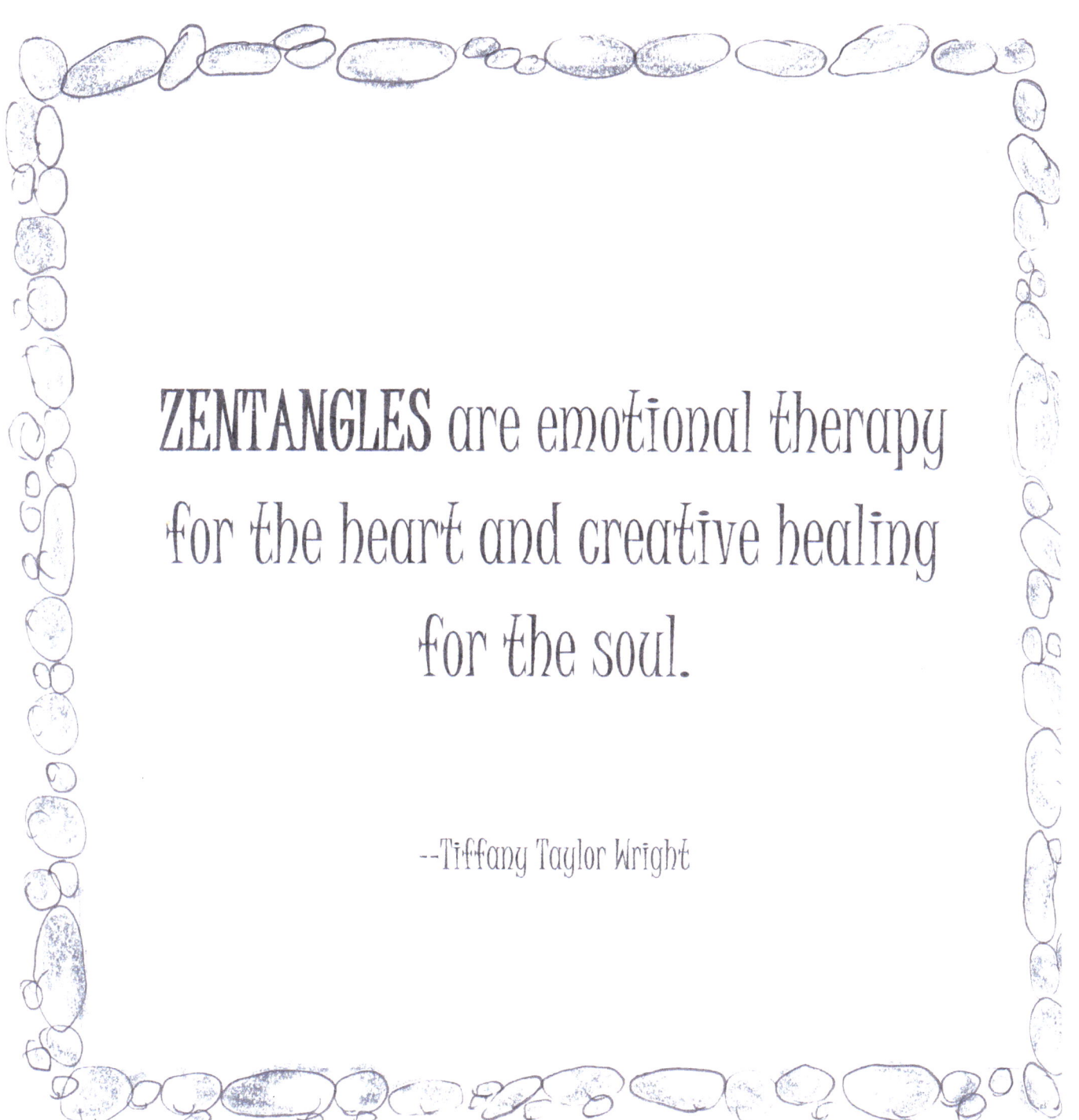

ZENTANGLES are emotional therapy for the heart and creative healing for the soul.

--Tiffany Taylor Wright

About the Author

Tiffany Taylor Wright is a native of Fresno, California and lives with her 19 year old daughter, Hayley. She has worked as a legal assistant for the last 30 years.

She enjoys spending as much time as she can at the Coast in Santa Cruz and Capitola, California. She is an avid beachcomber, searching for shells, interesting rocks and sand dollars for her collection.

She also loves to cook and try new recipes as well as shopping with her daughter. Tiffany enjoys refinishing old furniture by painting and decorating it to breathe new life into an old piece.

Tiffany has enjoyed creating art and trying new mediums in art from a very early age.

"My life, my soul, my art is the best of me."

- Tiffany Taylor Wright

Tiffany can be reached at twright62@sbcglobal.net.

CONCLUSION

In closing I would like to add that Zentangling can be done by anyone. All you need are a few simple tools - a sketchpad, black ink pens and watercolor pencils or markers. Whatever interests you.

Whether you think you are artistic or not, you can relax and draw a beautiful piece. The great thing is there are no mistakes in Zentangling, that's part of the fun.

There are lots of great websites and how-to's on YouTube to help you along the way and give you inspiration.

Give it a try! You will see how relaxing it can be and take you away from your day-to-day routine if even for a little while at a time.

I hope you have enjoyed this book as much as I have enjoyed creating it.

-Tiffany Taylor Wright

www.ingramcontent.com/pod-product-compliance
Lightning Source LLC
Chambersburg PA
CBHW050755180526
45159CB00003B/1467